Deep, Blue, Heavenly Seas

...A Retreat for Your Soul

Deep, Blue, Heavenly Seas

...A RETREAT FOR YOUR SOUL

25 Hawaiian-Inspired Spiritual Practices
to Help You Live Your Life
and Leave Your Legacy

MELISSA HECKMAN, MSW

ISBN: 978-0-9863816-3-8 Print
        978-0-9863816-4-5 eBook

Contact Information:
Melissa Heckman
P.O. Box 733
Lafayette, CA 94549-0733
Visit: MelissaHeckman.com
Email: MLHECKMAN2003@YAHOO.COM

DEDICATION

It is with a heart full of appreciation that I dedicate this book to my spiritual teachers. They come in many forms, from beloved family and friends, to wise saints and sages, to tiny and winged creatures, to the tall, soaring Hawaiian coconut trees, to art, music, seashells, the ocean, and life's miracle moments. This book is ultimately dedicated to all of life.

ACKNOWLEDGMENTS

I will do my best to acknowledge the individuals who inspire me beyond measure.

As divine timing would have it, my first writing coach and editor, Linda Joy Myers, president of the National Association of Memoir Writers and author of four books, showed up at the perfect time. She helped me focus when I needed to most.

A lovely friend, Susan L'Heaureaux, author of *California Stories*, also provided me with editing tips and writing guidance. I cannot express enough appreciation for her lessons and support.

Another lovely angel in human form appeared when I needed more editing help—Tricia Linden, international banker by day and spiritual romance author by night. She is the author of five books including *Dreaming in Moonlight*.

Two brilliant friends from my long standing San Francisco book club, Trisha O'Neil and Christine Owner, provided feedback, ideas, and crucial edits.

My wonderful mother, author, and teacher Pamela Hooper-Poland, has always encouraged me to express my creativity, to dance, to read out loud, to sing out loud, and to try new things. Her Southern sense of humor never ceases to crack me up. She touched my Southern heart recently when she gave me a book called *Butter My Butt and Call Me a Biscuit*. I flip through it laughing—and feel blessed to have a mother like her. I am proud to say that my mama-san, or mama-roo, has penned two children's novels. The greatest gift that she ever gave to me, beyond her immense love, was taking me to live in Hawaii as a young girl.

I also honor Dr. Reverend Patricia Keel. I appreciate her for praying powerfully with me, for opening Unity of Berkeley to me for speaking opportunities, and for reassuring me about teaching my life coaching workshops. She also encouraged creative expression and helped me to accept life as a prayer, always answered.

Author Wayne Dyer's teaching helped me establish the foundation I needed to accept myself as a spiritual being in the world. His words conveyed the messages I needed to hear to change my life—from the inner to the outer. Book after book, page by page, I would devour the lessons and inspirations. His work really motivated me to make concrete changes in my life. Mr. Dyer helped me shed anxiety and claim my goodness. He inspired me to row my own boat. He also provided the stable male voice of wisdom, confidence, and inspiration I had missed because of the early death of my father.

Authors Gerald Jampolsky, M.D., and Diane Cirincione, Ph.D., taught me about the power of forgiveness and how to move through loss and grief with the principles of Attitudinal Healing (derived from *A Course In Miracles*). I began applying Attitudinal Healing earnestly around 2005. I started off taking classes at the International Center for Attitudinal Healing—the center founded by Jerry in 1975. Shortly after starting the classes, I also became a volunteer. It was then that I began to understand and accept my tragic losses once and for all. As a result of my healing I became clear about the life I truly desired to be living. Soon thereafter I started teaching my life coaching workshops at the center as a guest speaker. I eventually became Director of Dr. Jampolsky's legendary healing programs. One of the things I am most proud of was enhancing the clinical therapy program and working with the clinical interns.

I will never forget the day I went to Jerry and Diane's home. I sat in the living room with these two New Thought spiritual icons, on their gorgeous houseboat in Sausalito, California. The expansive San Francisco Bay and a large breathtaking statue of Kuan Yin, the Chinese goddess of compassion, were in the background. Jerry and Diane led us in prayer. Then I told them about growing up in Hawaii and my desire to return there in the future to open a healing retreat center. I further explained that I wanted, in my first book, to convey something of a retreat experience for readers. Diane said they spend about half of the year in the same city where I grew up, Kailua. I silently affirmed, "Miracles are everywhere. Thank you, God." They patiently looked through every page of the first rough draft of my book. I kid you not—they looked through *every page* of the first rough draft even pausing to make nice comments, ask me questions, and make gentle suggestions. (We all know the first rough draft of anything should not be shared. I have since learned the value of re-writing the re-written, then re-writing more.) But their kindness in this instance tells you a lot about the loving presence of this wise and beautiful couple, successful authors who speak before audiences across the globe.

I knew how fortunate I was in those glorious moments as I tried to be present to what was occurring. To put it mildly, it was a monumental spiritual experience to witness both the outpouring of love and the receptivity of my own heart. Diane said, "This is such a lovely and unique book. We love it. Jerry, we can see this book being sold in the Honolulu airport bookstores, can't we?" Jerry agreed. They also suggested that their friend, Wayne Dyer (the one and only spiritual person I ever felt googly-eyed about) might be able to help support my book. I welcomed that gesture. As I had already felt my cup running over, I decided to let spirit hold that possibility for me. The generous support of Jerry and Diane gave me an even greater sense of purpose and mission.

After several repeat hugs and many thank-yous, I walked confidently out of their front door and strolled down the quaint boardwalk, noting the vast array of large teal and cobalt blue color flower pots. Like the abundant daisies, succulents, and lavender in those pots, I too was overflowing with life. I felt confident, thinking that no matter what it takes, I will finish this book to help others live out their life purpose—just as Jerry and Diane helped to hold that space for me. Everything was syncing up back then, and my life has felt very much in rhythm with the entire universe ever since. I acknowledge Jerry and Diane as my mentors and as role models.

I am grateful to the Unity New Thought teachings on positive practical spirituality and for Kailua Unity, Windward Unity, Unity of Berkeley, and Unity of Walnut Creek for all opportunities given to me to lead in those respective spiritual centers. I have participated as a Sunday Services Guest Speaker, Workshop Teacher, Prayer Chaplain, Platform Leader, and Meditation Leader. Unity recognizes and accepts people from all faiths and non-faiths, all religions and non-religions. Unity affirms people as they are and helps people expand their consciousness for the greater good of humanity. Unity is not fear based; rather, it is love centered, and that is mainly why I am drawn to the teachings. I am immensely appreciative for all that I have gained through Unity.

I owe a great deal of gratitude to my beloved soul-sister friend Christine Snyder, who perished in 9-11. She introduced me to the fun side of Hawaii and to a deeper part of myself. She also enjoyed New Thought teachings. Her friendship, strength, energy—and her loss—motivate me to get moving for the greater good in the world. She had a way of saying, "Get going, girlfriend," and her spirit continues to emanate this message as powerfully as ever.

The untimely death of my biological father, Thomas Willard Heckman, has been the most catastrophic event of my life. It caused me profound sadness and devastation deep within my being. The gifts from this loss, however, have included serious reflection, early personal deconstruction, and great appreciation for life.

My long time friend from Hawaii, a true yogi Goddess, Leana Levinsohn, has been a pillar of friendship and sisterhood. She embodies the "Aloha Spirit," and I am immensely grateful for her depth of being and for knowing when to breathe with me.

Many wonderful friends have supported me along the way—Kim McGovern with her strong spirituality, humor, and love; the entire brilliant and lively San Francisco book club gals; über talented Susan Szabo with her art and enthusiasm for life; and Mary Gutierrez, with prayer and loving friendship. Roselle Nottage and her daughter, Makamae, thoughtfully donated their support with edits for the Hawaiian terminology.

Jenny Dyer and Tina Dyer also gave generously as well when I stayed with them in Hawaii, in their respective beautiful homes. Both Jenny and Tina first introduced me to Unity in the late 1980s and took me to my first Unity service where Wally Amos, the famous "cookie man," was singing a song that went something like, "If the cookie man can, you can too…" I had to greatly respect a "church" that held so much joy and humor. Yet it did not feel like any church I had ever attended in the South. The experience was lively, authentic, and warm. Back then my agnostic beliefs were not ready to be transformed, however. Years later I would come to know Unity as more of a creative spiritual center.

My partner, Paul Kohut, has been my saving grace through so much during the writing of this book. He is a brilliant engineer and musician. He has been supportive, patient, and my technical "Mr. Fix It." He also cooked many gourmet meals as I typed away. I am grateful for his understanding, kindness, and his love.

The talented team at 1106 Design, led by Michele DeFilippo, held my hand and guided me through the last and most critical edits and the final stages of the book writing and design process. For their high level of professionalism and sincere desire to help me create a great book, I am appreciative. A very special kudos goes to my editor Doran Hunter who I cannot thank enough.

I have also been fueled by the master teaching, authorship, and wisdom energies of Marianne Williamson, Oprah Winfrey, Gloria Steinem, Louise Hay, Deepak Chopra, Eckhart Tolle, Thich Nhat Hanh, Jon Kabat-Zinn, Eknath Easwaran, Eric Butterworth, Louise Hay, Esther and Jerry Hicks, Maya Angelou, and Madam Pele (The Hawaiian Fire Goddess).

There are innumerable clients, patients, colleagues, students, interns, and volunteers who I have had the opportunity to work with and serve as a Life Coach and as a Clinical and Medical Social Worker. They have gifted me with their upsets, stories, healings, successes, losses, laughter, and dreams. There have been insights and sharing which have moved me deeply and helped me to heal and grow. Holding sacred court with them on our respective journeys has been awesome. They all inspire me to continue to evolve myself for the planet.

Lastly, I owe much to Hawaii ʻaina (land of Hawaii) for my healing and life inspiration. Mahalo (thank you) for the sacred time I have spent being held by the perfect crystalline healing waters, whispered to by the wise bamboo and playful coconut trees, and being sung to by the delightful early morning birdsongs of doves cooing. Mahalo for the soul-stirring energy of the Fire Goddess Pele, for being lovingly embraced by the spectacular sunrise, and gently hugged by the warm tropical breezes. Mahalo for the honus (Hawaiian sea turtles), the abundant flora and fauna, the ancient Hawaiian lava tubes, succulent Haden mangos, and perfectly timed passing rain showers. Mahalo for the towns I love most: Lanikai, Kailua, Waialua, Haleiwa, Makawao, Kula, Paia, Hana, and Lahaina. Mahalo for the marvelous Monkey Pod trees, for the secret seashell beaches, for the glorious swimming with dolphins adventure, for the magical whale sightings, and the continued anticipation of new discoveries.

The mana (energy) of Hawaii ʻaina has been my main medicine—the prescription that led me to my healing. I honor and respect all that is Hawaii.

AUTHOR'S INTRODUCTION

In the early 1980s, around the age of eleven, I attended intermediate school on the island of Oahu in a town called Aiea. The name, like most Hawaiian words, has many vowels in it. From the very beginning, I had fun getting to know this new vocabulary as my family drove from the Honolulu airport up to the Aiea hillside for the first time. As we went, I enjoyed trying to pronounce the names of local streets and exotic words on random signs, but it was obvious that my Southern accent was mangling what I suspected were beautifully musical sounds. We hooted and howled together at my silly antics. I had a lot to learn about the Hawaiian language and local culture.

My step-grandfather, the late Marine Corps Colonel James A. Poland, was stationed at the Camp Smith military installation in Aiea. His title "Commander of the Pacific Fleet" commanded immediate respect. When with his family, he was kind, funny, and easy-going. Within a few weeks of attending Aiea Intermediate School, someone had stolen my book bag out of the girl's locker room. I was shocked, crushed, and very much disturbed. While my grandfather helped me in his usual joking manner, he also had a serious message, as he usually did. This time the message was, "Get rid of that Southern accent and get a tan. You need to befriend the locals, then they will take care of you—and they won't kill you on the last day of school which is called, by the way, 'Kill Haole Day.'" After a pause, I heard him chuckle as he walked out of the living room. I knew what he meant about acquiring new friends, but I was worried, very worried, about getting the crap kicked out of me just for trying. The term "Haole" stands for "outsider" or "non-local." That was the first of my life lessons about assimilating into one of the most beautiful and colorful melting pots in the world. Thankfully, I was allowed to skip the last day of school that year, for my whole family feared I might not have learned the local mentality well enough to keep from getting my scrawny okole (butt) punted off Halawa Heights all the way to the Haleakala summit on Maui. The "killing" was a bit of hype, but the fear of a ruckus ensuing remained in the back of my mind nonetheless.

Remembering grandpa's unequivocal remarks, the next day I changed one of my classes and signed up for a Hawaiian studies class. It saved me. I also worked on my tan and befriended the locals by ordering my lunch from the local food trucks. The food truck drivers were affectionately known as "The Manapua Men" because they sold the delicious sweet filled pork buns (manapua) that the kids went crazy (pupule) for. From my Southern roots, I knew that food has its way of connecting people. At the trucks I devoured Asian noodles, candy, and pickled mango. Hanging out by the food trucks, plus equal parts naivety and boldness, brought me closer to the local population indeed. There I could overhear conversations and interpret how to hang out and be cool, local style. I learned how to correctly pronounce street names and towns. I listened acutely. I learned to adapt the local dialect known as "Hawaiian Pidgin," a type of Hawaiian Creole English. People shared their food with me and offered me opportunities to try new things like salty plum seeds. I loved the immersion and adopted all of it without reservation. My understanding and respect for the island culture grew. The locals became protective of me as I became a little more like them—just as Gramps said they would.

I also enjoyed learning about the basics of the Hawaiian language in my Hawaiian studies class. I loved the way all of those vowels rolled off my tongue. Hawaiian grammar is rather complex despite the fact that there are only eight consonants, five short vowels, and five long vowels.

As the years passed, I fully assimilated into the local culture and gained many friends despite remaining a sun-burned, freckle-faced, bony Haole. My friends grew to be a glorious mix of Haole, Hawaiian, Japanese, Chinese, Filipino, Samoan, Fijian, and Hapa (of mixed ethnic heritage). After I completed the school year in Aiea, we moved to the Windward side of Oahu, first to Kaneohe then to Kailua. All of that was the beginning of my eternal love affair with Hawaii.

I have decided to share simple Hawaiian terms with you in my writing because I want to show my regard to the Hawaiian culture, and in a small way help to preserve a wonderful language and way of life.

Hawaii is incredibly stunning. Yet it is more than physical beauty, much more. It is more than what television has shown us—the Brady Bunch's visit to the Big Island, The Skipper, Gilligan, The Professor, Mary Ann, Ginger, and Mr. and Mrs. Thurston Howell III. It is even so much more than Hawaii Five-0 and Magnum, P.I. It is more than the quintessential Mai Tai. More than plane loads of tourists flocking to fancy hotels. It is more than the ultimate destination wedding. It is more than a tropical golden tanned Hapa-Haole face, flower in her hair, gracing the cover of a glossy brochure. The essence of what I think of as "real Hawaii" is rich with spirit, that which we cannot see with the naked eye. It is a feeling, to be experienced within one's heart and soul. It is profound, humble, uncomplicated, forgiving, fresh, loving, neighborly, leisurely, and lively.

The twenty five chapters in this book are infused with Hawaiian terms (either the English or Hawaiian will be in parentheses). You will also find highlighted terms (not Hawaiian) that help to make important points. These are called out by using **bold**. Like a perfect Hawaiian sunrise or sunset sparkling on the ocean, beyond the visual—I hope the **intensity and magnification** helps the spiritual lessons and life practices **soak into your soul**.

Within each chapter I offer you resources that I playfully call "prescriptions," indicated with the "Rx" mark. They compliment the exercises and suggested practices. I strongly suggest that you **at least try the exercises** even if they seem challenging. Use them as ways to feel better and manage daily life. They are designed to ignite your learning, to help you grow, expand, and evolve. I have seen people experience a profound progression of growth and insight when they "fill the prescriptions" by practicing the exercises. As you work on your own, you will reap great rewards and become the **master artist** of your life, co-creating with the entire universe.

TABLE OF CONTENTS

Act II: Diving In

Act III. Riding the Wave to the Shore

FOREWORD

Let's face it: Sometimes what is preached in spiritual self-help books comes across as inauthentic, leaving many readers turned off. As a result, even excellent spiritual advice is ignored. We think you'll find this book to be different. If you are spiritually aware or spiritually curious, this book can help tune you into, and turn you onto, powerful ways of thinking, acting, and being in the world.

Few authors are able to write from a place of deep heart connection that demonstrates a combination of creativity and a desire to sincerely serve the reader. As she serves as your guide through her mind expanding and heart opening process, you will find Melissa's writing to be kind and genuine. She gives you inspiring questions and exercises with a unique "trip to Hawaii." You are encouraged to be introspective with questions and exercises, along with her interwoven personal stories, the carefully placed and perfectly themed quotes, and relevant tidbits of Hawaiian culture.

Hawaii is home to a diverse population representing the melting pot of the world. The spiritual landscapes of Hawaii, along with the essence of the "Aloha Spirit" found in the pages of this book, will resonate with most people. In these pages, Melissa has found a unique way to combine her eighteen years' experience as a clinical social worker helping people from all walks of life, her expanded spirituality, and her obvious love of Hawaii. She carefully integrates her own stories of tragedy, triumph, and healing as if she is sitting next to you on a white, sandy beach having a heart-to-heart talk with you.

Deep, Blue Heavenly Seas contains spiritual practices in each chapter where you will find clearly defined mental steps and exercises. Melissa's gentle voice and nudging creates a space for you to feel guided every step of the way. She serves as your partner on your own unique journey. Together these are more than "prescriptions." The lessons are more like an advanced course on wise living. The subject moves from death and dying to life and living, with key spiritual concepts throughout the book: Embrace your fears of dying so that you can truly live that which you plan to leave in the world.

One memorable chapter on the process of forgiveness includes exceptional journaling assignments to help you accelerate your personal growth. This challenging subject is delivered in such a way that most anyone can be motivated to complete the exercises. We especially appreciate how Melissa weaves in the principles of Attitudinal Healing, the practices which we have spent our life dedicated to teaching.

This book is a retreat for your soul, practical and instructive. What better way to open our hearts and our minds than to be on a "vacation" while doing so. As we read segments and shared these stories together, we found ourselves feeling "lit up" with renewed zest for living our legacy. Since we spend significant time in Hawaii, we know the deep feeling of "aloha" that has been captured in these pages—a feeling that should be spread far and wide. Get ready to take a transformational trip of a lifetime!

Gerald Jampolsky, M.D., Diane Cirincione, Ph.D.

Co-authors of *A Mini Course for Life*

Act I: Preparing to Dive

CHAPTER 1: WELCOME

Aloha (welcome) to a retreat for your soul. This experience can be a unique journey, and much like the rest of your life, you have a few options—**you can play it deep or play it shallow.** As my mom used to say, "You don't have time to dilly dally" and "the world is your oyster." With that in mind, I invite you to take the plunge chapter by chapter to discover the stunning, shiny pearls of your greatest self. Although I believe it is important to be playful in life, I also feel it's essential to dive into your soul ('uhane) on very deep, intimate levels and authentically live your life from that place. "That place" can also be viewed as your consciousness or spirituality. Spiritual unfolding is a compelling and delightful evolution of your true self—when you desire it and allow it to be the guiding force of your life. **It is an inner adventure, your own "inside job," grounded on insights and awareness.** It is a shift in your mindset and in the way you live your life every day of the week—even moment to moment.

One of the most remarkable things I've ever done is to sort out who I AM—my inner world could be a rather confusing place until I opened myself up to spiritual living. My purpose and passion has been to help others create more peace and to live out their life purpose. I hold an enormous space for knowing that you can rise to your full potential and live a beautifully successful life. I will help you envision that, define that, and create that.

Life teaches the value of learning, unlearning, opening, and surrendering, and this practice will parallel that process. It is divided into three acts and 25 chapters. Each Act is written to help you build your consciousness, release negative energies, and change unhealthy thought patterns to enable you to claim your highest self in your own spiritual terms. I encourage you to give your own names to the concepts discussed in this book, to invent your own spiritual vocabulary if you wish. If the use of the term "spirituality" is uncomfortable for you I encourage you to view spiritual experience as a process of gaining life mastery. Each chapter will help you see yourself from different perspectives and guide you to return to an innate sense of who you are—so you can free yourself to live your ultimate life.

Act I: Preparing to Dive provides background information, inspiration, and motivation for you to set the stage for your own success. Each chapter progressively helps you prepare for the next. The instructive exercises will help you to identify your legacy (the blessings you wish to leave behind after you die) and begin drafting your life purpose. Act I will also help you release old stories and patterns that impede living your life purpose. In addition you will be asked to let some ideas percolate within. Then you will be invited to begin some pre-contemplative exercises that you will return to in later chapters.

Act II: Diving In will focus on strategies to get you in touch with your spiritual core however you define it for yourself. This will help you deepen your awareness of your inner self. These chapters are designed to help you immerse yourself in understanding and tame the ego, so you can live more from your true essence and heed your soul calling. Several of these chapters submerge you even deeper, helping you traverse the abyss of ego.

Act III: Riding the Wave to the Shore helps you solidify your legacy so you can become crystal clear on your life purpose and begin to consciously live it and celebrate it. You are then provided additional tools for fully embracing and living out your life goals and aspirations.

I am here to support you as you open yourself up to inspirational ideas that I have gleaned from my coaching, clinical, and spiritual practices, as well as from my personal life lessons—the good, the bad, even the catastrophic. I will also demonstrate what I learned from living in Hawaii and from the wisdom of the beautiful Hawaiian culture; throughout, I have made use of relevant Hawaiian terminology where I thought it conveyed something essential. Everything has been carefully integrated to help serve your greatest needs. At times you will find that I have reiterated points from earlier sections. All of this serves to help you establish essential life practices to last well beyond your reading of the book.

MY EVOLVEMENT

This process began at a point in my life when I knew I needed to make a serious shift mainly in my career but also with relationships. It happened after I quit a job where I felt miserable, followed by a dramatic breakup. I responded to a thundering call from deep within me saying, "Hey, darling, go in and find your true self. No more playing small." Clinical Social Work alone was not fulfilling me, and I knew that obtaining a psychotherapy license and opening a private practice would not satisfy me either. I had a great desire to express more of my creativity and to unleash my greatest gifts, and I wanted to help others do the same. I started to read and study spiritual masters in addition to researching this new thing called Life Coaching. I started to distance myself from negative, condescending, and competitive people. I nurtured my self-esteem in new ways. I learned to love being alone. I started to really listen to the inner voice of my true self. I fell in love with prayer and meditation. I dabbled more with art. I trained for my first marathon and completed it. I started to dream bigger and take the necessary steps to live from a completely different mindset once and for all.

I started to embrace Life Coaching principles which resonated with the strengths-based aspects of my clinical work. That's when so many wonderful things began unfolding with my work and personal relationships. Life began to feel more fluid and gentle, and I began to feel naturally radiant. I learned so much when I began to open up and see how others were achieving authentic happiness. I began to think from a plenteous frame of mind which forced me to choose differently in all areas of my life. I learned how to apply my unique

EXERCISE

If you don't have one yet, buy yourself a new journal solely dedicated to this work. Put your name in your journal and keep it in a sacred place. You may want to buy one that fits into your purse or backpack so you can have it readily available. Decorate it as you see fit and write yourself a little love note dedicating the journal as a treasured gift to yourself. Draw and play along with your responses to the exercises as well. And by all means, use color to express yourself too! Maybe having a tin of colorful markers or pencils would be inspiring next to your journal. You know yourself best, so set yourself up for a profound and playful experience.

skills and talents and creativity to help others. I created a life coaching program and a life coaching workbook. I honored my clinical background for giving me the foundation to become a good coach. I also began connecting with people and places that were in alignment with my true values, which allowed me to gain more opportunities to teach and coach from the workbook. It felt like tectonic shifts were taking place in all areas of my life. I was achieving significant results, and I was so excited I knew I had to share it. Over the years the workbook has evolved into the spiritual practices described in this book—a retreat for your soul. Each chapter helps you flow through the process much as if you were in one of my intensive coaching workshops.

As I enhance my coaching program, I remain a clinician in a medical setting. Many of the patients I work with have complex medical needs and are nearing the end of life, and I serve as a guide for them. I help them cope with stress, change, and loss, as well as to face the inevitable. I love my work and it seems the coaching and clinical practice are a perfect match. The days are now more effortless and effervescent for me—yet that's not to say I don't have bad days. I do. The great thing is that I don't have nearly as many of them as I had in the past. I am not going to pretend that I am any better than you or set myself in a separate class than you just because of a few college degrees or having become an author. We are equals. I have something to share in the form of this teaching, and you have something to share of significant value to others as well. For now I get to share my revelations, prescriptions, and program with you so you can learn to live your best life and then perhaps launch your unique vision to share with others also.

LANIKAI

Lanikai is a pristine beach on the island of Oahu in the Hawaiian Islands and a place I find very special. In the Hawaiian language Lanikai Uli means "Deep Blue Heavenly Seas." I was born in North Carolina, but it was on the beaches of Oahu, mainly Lanikai, where I grew up. I've enjoyed intimate beach walks, joyous and profound beach talks, spectacular full moons, beach dances, snorkeling with turtles, sunrise meditation, sunrise yoga, prayer, kayaking, surfing, Smash ball, boat rides, a sinking boat adventure, sailing on catamarans, picnics, hikes, journaling, and many miracle moments around Lanikai. There were times when I stood on Lanikai beach feeling like I was in heaven. The deep blue-green and crystal clear healing waters hold the essence of spiritual wisdom from the earth and sea and help me know the deep truth of who I am and my purpose for being. I believe that everyone's soul resonates with certain places. Do you have a place like this?

LEGACY

I offer you the opportunity to explore these exercises and principles to **reveal parts of yourself that are dying to live**. I want to help you fully embrace the life you dream about, the life you deserve to be living. You will be asked to examine your legacy (the blessings you want to leave behind when you die) as an essential deep inquiry to help you live your life focused, with passion and on purpose.

STATE OF MIND

Deep, Blue, Heavenly Seas has become a state of mind for me, a paradise I can return to over and over again in my head and hold in my heart even when the waters of life get rough. The practices I've used are outlined for you in the chapters ahead—they keep me centered and they can do the same for you. This experience is intended to give you a levity boost, inner tremors, and an "ecstatic uplift." I invite you to flow…allow your entire essence to free itself and boldly **dream your life**, the way you really want to be living it, **alive!**

You are the expert on you. Although I share my insights, stories, reference others, cite, and suggest, the most important element of the teaching is about helping you manage your mind and connect with your intuition. I propose that you tap into your life inspirations and define your own paradise as well. Be daring and fearless with this, and allow your visions to move across the movie screen of your mind in vivid Technicolor.

"The only courage you ever need is the courage to fulfill the dreams of your own life."
—*Oprah*

The practices offered are designed to help you open your mind in order to live a more authentically powerful life. Have you given thought to how you might claim your authentic power, your truth for being, and heed your soul-calling? What kind of things do you think could help you with areas in your life where you feel you have lost your purpose?

SETTING

Although Hawaii is my go-to spiritual backdrop, you can choose your own special place that inspires you as you reflect and complete the exercises. You will benefit by having a comfortable setting where you can reflect, write, and contemplate your life. So feel free to define your physical space and let your **imagination** traipse the globe, or consider visiting a local lake, or park, or even your own backyard.

SPIRITUALITY

You don't need to be "spiritual" or have a particular religious belief to benefit from the practices. The practices are **steeped in love,** and love crosses all belief systems, borders, nationalities, and cultures. As I've lead in group meditations, "Love does not discriminate, so allow your love to flow from the center of your being and envision sending it out to those around you, your community, and the entire world. Imagine loving, healing energy reaching anyone who might be suffering." If you are an agnostic, searching, have no need for defining a "God," call yourself a Jew, Muslim, Buddhist, Christian, Hindu, or other, all is well. Just come with an **open mind and heart,** and explore these teachings by whatever term you wish. I do not come from a fundamentalist perspective. There is no priggishness in this book. Nor is there any room for stiff-necked preaching in my teaching. I highly value love, peace, and partnership. This is not a top-down model. I want to co-create with you, for the greater good of humanity. Humanity leaves no one out. I have gathered together my teaching with the intention that it convey the energy of love and authentic power in every syllable of every word that I have written.

These are my truths. I also believe they are universal truths connected like a molecule chain from a common global emotion. At times, I may use the terms "Soul," "Spirit," "Spirituality," "God," "Goddess," "Higher Power," "Divinity,"

"Buddha," "Christ," "Divine Mind," "Nature," "Consciousness," "Mana," "Energy," "Life," and "Love." In essence, each refers to the mysterious Source of "all that is." Take a moment and go back and put each of those terms in this sentence and see how it feels to you: "We are all one _____." Can you think of how we might all be innately associated? Try not to let language trip you up. Go beyond the name. Often two different words mean the same thing, such as mountain (in English) and mauka (in Hawaiian). But it is clear that the object is the same even though it can have different names. Whether one is Hindu, Buddhist, Christian, Jew, Muslim, or _____ (you name it), we are after one thing—the ultimate dimension. It is beyond a name.

SOMETHING LARGER

I used to consider myself to be a spiritual skeptic. However, I began to realize that "religion" and "spirituality" are very different. Once I was clued into this, I freed myself to design my own sense of spirituality and to connect with the God of my understanding. In Hawaii, I felt connected to nature. There was something in the elements that felt like home after I had stripped the rigid dogmas of my youth from my psyche. Back then, like many people, I was taught that I was bad by nature. I thought "God" was a white-bearded man seated among the clouds in the sky whom no one could see. I felt I needed to prove myself to Him, but I eventually began to open up to the many possibilities of what the term "God" could mean…thanks to my time in Hawaii and as I opened myself up to new ways of thinking and believing. I am no longer a skeptic about spirituality, but I still do not consider myself to be religious. There is nothing wrong with this spiritual-but-not-religious perspective. I know many people who have made this shift from religious to spiritual. The main idea here is for you to connect with, or re-connect with, the **essential YOU** and feel part of Something Larger, however you define it. Spirituality can also be viewed as having a sense of grace—an energy or higher power greater than yourself. Once you get in touch with it, and stay in touch with it, it moves in through—and *as*—you.

EXERCISE

Go ahead and create a sacred space for you to reflect and to write. This can be as simple as claiming a corner of a room, with a comfortable chair and an end table, or desk space for yourself.

"Spirituality helps us regain our mental equipoise, self-confidence and a positive attitude to move forward."
—*Amma*

THE JOURNAL

Much like a diary, keeping a journal is a writing tool that can be therapeutic and help ignite a creative process. It can help you express emotion, reduce stress, formulate ideas, and be a source of comfort. In a way, I think it can also serve as an unconditional friend whom you can tell anything to. Try to honor your journal and the moments you have with it.

THE SPACE

It will benefit you to declare your own physical space, giving yourself a type of **sanctuary** for the work you will be doing. This is where you **plug in and connect** with your innermost desires.

Also, you might want to follow sequentially each part and chapter since I've designed them to be gradual and progressive; but there is no right or wrong way to take in the teaching. You could also allow a slow six month experience if you map out the chapters giving approximately one week per chapter so you can take in the exercises slowly and allow yourself sufficient time for reflection and application. No matter your method or pace, I hope you will become saturated with creative energy unfolding miracles in **your luminous life**.

For your space, I encourage you to use simple decorations and elements from nature such as seashells, pinecones, dried leaves, flowers, or whatever you are called to gather. The idea is to create a place you can retreat to and call your own. If possible it should be private and without distractions (such as no television, computer, or phone). You really want to have this time to go inside and to be free of outside influences while you are doing the work. Try this next exercise to help you explore your readiness:

EXERCISE

Freely journal your thoughts on the following questions:

1. How do I currently define "God" or "spirituality" in my life?

2. What gives me meaning in my life?

3. Am I open to explore my own wounds and scars, so I can live the life I truly want to be living? If not, what gets in my way?

4. How much do I truly want to live an authentically powerful and magnificent life and what could that look like for me?

"Twenty years from now you will be more disappointed by the things that you didn't do than by the ones you did do. So throw off the bowlines. Sail away from the safe harbor. Explore. Dream. Discover."
—*Mark Twain*

CHAPTER 2: CONNECTING

Growing up in Hawaii I learned how important it is to connect with the unfolding moment and with people. I did not seek this knowledge, and no one taught it to me. At some point, nature took a hold of me, and I fell into the arms of the verdant landscape and into the Spirit of Aloha which guided me to experience life differently than I had in the South where I was born. In Hawaii there were many times when nature tapped on my shoulder and guided me to take a different path in my life. I was being plugged into life, and over the years I've increased the voltage by increasing my awareness of spirit within me and all around me.

Do you feel like you want to plug in or **connect more deeply** with your life?

SHIFTS

At the age of eleven, stepping across the airport breezeway at the Honolulu airport for the first time, I felt the warm air caress my body. It was swift, thick air, and fluid. Those breezes left a permanent imprint on my naïve soul; they would visit me many times to help me heal. Throughout my adult life, I have practiced my own inner work, which helps me now to serve others and navigate the winds of life with more grace and ease. My only wish is that I could have learned my lessons sooner, and that I'd had a guide like I want to be for you.

EXERCISE

Think of times in your life where you experienced shifts in your identity. Remember important milestones, such as when you received your driving license, or when you graduated from high school or college, or when you married, moved, or had children. Perhaps you can think back to how you might have had to let go of an older part of you to more fully embrace the transformed person you were becoming. Most of us were not consciously aware of changes in our identity early in our lives, but we can use our reflections about the past to help us learn to be more aware today.

Inner work is essentially about healing your past and coping with changes, by whatever means work for you. This could include reading self-help books, attending workshops and retreats, or engaging with professional talk therapy. Yes, there will be suffering, but my goal is to help you **heal your suffering…to live through it and learn from it.** With this type of conscious healing, you can connect more deeply with your life.

I feel strongly that it is my kuleana (sacred responsibility) to help others heal. Notice I did not say I think I should "fix" people. That is definitely not my purpose. What I offer is an intimate sharing, profound insights, as well as tools to help you think and choose differently, giving you a greater capacity for your own healing.

The events of 9-11 also catapulted me into healthier realms of living and inspired me to connect with others in more meaningful ways. I lost a very dear friend, Christine Snyder, who perished on flight 93 that went down near Pittsburgh. The loss of Christine helped me grow to appreciate all of my relationships on deeper levels and to start to think about what is truly important to me. I will share more about Christine in later sections. That experience also helped me see that there is a serious need for both individual and collective healing.

EXERCISE

In your journal, write a statement of intention explaining what you hope to get out of working through this process. It can look something like this, "I (name) intend to become more peace centered with my family, my work, and in all of my relationships." Or, "I (name) intend to get clear about my purpose and passion, and then focus on living it."

INTENTION

My intention is to guide you to open your **heart,** to **release,** to **forgive,** and to **appreciate** so you can enjoy the oceans of life. I hope to motivate you to live your truth and navigate your internal world so you can restructure your thinking and fall in love with your own life. I will help you move from living mostly in your head to coming from your heart and soul. **Are you ready to radiate and glow, sparkle and shine? Do you want to feel intimately connected with all of life, unfold the miracle of your pure potential, and live your mana (life force)?** In order

for you to set yourself up for success with this process, it will be helpful to organize yourself and set
your priorities.

GRATITUDE

Creating a mind full of gratitude is one of the highest
spiritual practices. In terms of preparing yourself,
it is important to connect in gratitude with where
you are in your life right now. Having some type of
daily gratitude or appreciation practice
will help you start your days off on the right note. It
can also help you build more moments of appreciation into your day.

Affirm out loud, "Thank you, thank you, thank
you, life, for this day." In Hawaii we say, "Mahalo,"
for thank you. Affirm, "Mahalo, mahalo, mahalo,
life, for this day."

Affirm out loud, "I am grateful for all that I am,
all that I have, and all that is on the way."

EXERCISE

Try the following gratitude practices and
see which ones help you the most.

1. Upon waking each morning, as you are
   getting out of your bed, consciously
   place your feet on the floor. Set mindfulness in motion here by feeling all
   four corners of your feet on the floor.
   As you sit on the edge of your bed,
   state your gratitude for the day. Set
   your intention for the day by visualizing success for the main tasks you
   will embark upon for the day.

2. Answer the following questions in your
   journal. These help you appreciate your
   life and create more meaning in your
   life now. Ask yourself: What would I
   do if I only had one week left to live?
   What would I do if I only had one
   month left to live? What would I do if
   I only had one year left to live? What
   would I do if I had five years left to live?
   What would I do if I only had one life
   left to live?

3. At the close of each day before you get
   into bed, state specific things you are
   grateful for from the day.

"Why not on first awakening remind ourselves that this is a fresh new day, full of opportunities and fragrant with possibilities?"
—*Myrtle Fillmore*

CHAPTER 3: COME INSIDE.
THE HOUSE IS YOURS.

The 'aina (land) of Hawaii is very special in many ways. The position of the islands of Hawaii geographically makes it a vortex of spiritual energy—one among a number of such points throughout the world. These special places are the meeting points of lines of energy that have been mapped and calibrated. Sacred sites have been identified by humans throughout history and consistently fall along these lines with especially powerful areas of energy openings occurring at certain locations. The active volcanoes of the Big Island, also known as Hawaii (the largest of the islands), are jaw-dropping and heart-skipping to behold. This fiery show reminds us of our innate power and connection to nature—Mother Earth—our home. Of course I am not saying that we have volcanic powers. In this chapter I want you to feel into and connect with the essence of your inner most being and use nature to help you do that.

RETURN

In Hawaii we say "E komo mai. Nou ka hale" (Come inside. The house is yours). The spirit of aloha and the beauty of the land of Hawaii convey powerful

> ### EXERCISE
>
>
>
> Envision this—consider yourself on a rigorous hike leading deep into a tropical Hawaiian rain forest and to the top of a mountain. There will be moments of beauty as well as times of confusion on the path, running out of breath, slowing down, swimming through complete darkness in an ancient Hawaiian lava tube, painful scrapes and bruises, heat and thirst, wanting to turn back, getting drenched with passing rain storms. Finally, sunshine will break through the tree tops and there'll be glorious views at the top. No matter what, you keep going, knowing that the adventurous trip will be well worth your efforts.

messages that, when heeded, help you to return to **your true home, your loving nature,** and to your true self. You must go "in" to change the outer parts of your life. Allow nature to inspire you. When my fire was lit, inspired by my spiritual teachers and many walks along Hawaiian beaches, I began to make critical changes. I moved from embodying the pain and suffering from my early childhood and several tragic losses to embracing my potential for living a full and bounteous life. That's when my entire life started to return to its true purpose. Yours can too.

COURAGE

I recommend you give yourself ample quiet time to "be still and go inside" with each exercise. I've created them to help you get more comfortable with your inner self. Feel yourself there, wherever the experience takes you, whether it is in a guided imagery, poem, quote, art work, meditation, prayer, or journal entry. Try to **feel** your feelings, and move from your head to your heart. This work is often challenging so feel whatever arises and **be gentle with yourself along the way**. Also it is essential to be raw and **truthful** to yourself, even if it is uncomfortable. **This work takes courage and great daring**. This is the path of learning—moving through discomfort or unease to something new and different.

THE ROYAL GARDEN TEMPLE OF YOU

This coaching experience serves to help nurture your mind, body, and soul. It is intended to be thought provoking, meditative, playful, and transformative, helping you design and maintain the royal garden temple of you. You get to be everything from the owner-architect to the caretaker. As you work through these chapters, you will be nourished with each pupu (appetizer) offered in the form of quotes and messages and with the larger portions of the full luau (traditional Hawaiian feast)—deepening exercises and stories that have been carefully prepared in each chapter. My wish for

---

EXERCISE

Ask yourself the following questions then write your answers in your journal.

1. How do I currently describe "the gardens of me"?

2. How do I want to define "the gardens of me"?

3. What would "the gardens of me" look like and feel like at their peak ripeness?

4. What would my life be like if I were really singing and dancing to my own tune in my own bountiful garden?

you is that you **boldly open yourself to new dimensions of unfurling consciousness and find your inner compass** so you may ride out, from the vantage point of your highest self, every wave of life's stressors and changes.

Let nature help you tap into your true self. You can be the Queen or King ruling the lush gardens of you. Imagine stepping into the procession of your fresh and majestic life.

EXERCISE

Envision yourself strolling down the middle of two rows of tall coconut trees, dancing and twirling in tune with your spirit. The trees are swaying to your groove, and the rhythm of life is beating with your heartbeat.

"Though I may travel far I will meet only what I carry with me, for every man is a mirror. We see only ourselves reflected in those around us. Their attitudes and actions are reflections of our own.

The whole world and
its conditions has its
counterpart within us, All.
Turn the gaze inward…
correct yourself and your
world will change."
—*Kristin Zambucka*

CHAPTER 4: ALOHA SPIRIT

The Aloha Spirit is about the love of the 'aina (land) and the simple living and friendliness found in the varied cultures throughout the islands of Hawaii. The word "aloha" has many meanings, including, "welcome," "love," "mercy," "compassion," "pity," "greeting," "loved one," "to love," "to greet," "to hail."

At http://www.prideofmaui.com/blog/activities/best-things-hawaiian-culture.html I recently discovered that the Spirit of Aloha is actually part of Hawaiian state law! From the site: "The Hawaii Revised Statutes 5-7.5 acknowledges the Spirit of Aloha—as not just a philosophy, but also a law that all government officials and citizens (and visitors, too) are obligated to be in accordance with on a daily basis." Hawaii recognizes the Aloha Spirit as "the coordination of mind and heart within each person. It brings each person to the self. Each person must think and emote good feelings to others."

The natural beauty of Hawaii is included in my definition when I think of "Aloha Spirit." If you have ever seen a glorious sunrise from the top of Haleakala (the largest dormant volcano in the world) on the island of Maui, you will know what I mean about witnessing and feeling the miracle of aloha. That experience is truly an awakening for one's soul.

This section is about helping you to **wake up, and rise up,** to live from the deep truth of who you really are.

SPIRITUAL BEINGS

Before we go there… To help you know who you really are, you must know who or what you are *not*. It is important to know that the world teaches you to be materialistic, scientific, and physical. You are not only your physical body.

Your body is an aspect of who you are in the physical plane but the real you is not your body. Nor are you meant to be materially or scientifically centered. You have been taught to live from a cut-off aspect of your true self.

The following definitions from Merriam-Webster Online Dictionary help to make this point:

1. Spiritual is defined as, "Of, relating to, consisting of, or affecting the spirit: incorporeal."

2. Spirit is defined as, "The force within a person that is believed to give the body life, energy, and power: the inner quality or nature of a person."

3. Incorporeal is defined as, "Not corporeal: having no material body or form."

Like all of us, **you are a perfect spiritual being who happens to be having an imperfect human experience**.

Through immersion in the world, you forgot that your true essence is spiritual. Western culture denies, rejects, and represses spirituality. As a result, you live in illusions of who you are. Day in and day out you buy into society's standards, illnesses, rigidity, over consuming, and un-loving ways. Even the most highly spiritually evolved and self-actualized individuals continue to dance with this dichotomy of life. These ways of being are confusing, consuming, and concerning, but they are fast becoming old notions about how to live because more and more people are awakening to the truth.

It is a new day and you are well on your way to embracing new ways of viewing the world and of being in the world, more like the Aloha Spirit. It may take a while for these concepts to sink in, as it did for me, but once you understand them, you will begin to have a dramatically new experience of life.

When you get that you are first and foremost a spiritual being coming from an **all loving Source,** you begin to understand that upsets, pains, stressors, changes, losses, illnesses, diseases, and prognoses don't define you and will therefore have less control over you. Roles, titles, things, and material goods will begin to lose their meaning. You will come to know **love as an essential structure of the universe**, and that it flows through every person inasmuch as one desires it and surrenders to it.

It usually takes some kind of **soul searching** or **spiritual awakening** to know you are only temporarily in your physical body and you have a deeper purpose for living. Often such knowledge is gained when life challenges appear or when embracing a new way of living begins to shift you out of old patterns and belief systems. You start to wake up to **new levels of consciousness** and ways of being in the world. Then you find yourself being more present, loving, forgiving, at peace, less frazzled, more creative, less competitive, more connected, and less confused. You move into living from your true purpose, and you go from lost to found. You also come to know your **true self-worth, which is inward, spiritually-based, positive, connected, and accepting** versus living from attachments to self-worth from the outer, negative, separate, competitive, physical world.

In *Life Lessons* Elizabeth Kubler-Ross and David Kessler write,

> *"When we face the worst that can happen in any situation, we grow. When circumstances are at their worst, we can find our best. When we find the true meaning of these lessons, we also find happy, meaningful lives. Not perfect, but authentic. We can live life profoundly."*

They go on to say,

> *"Perhaps this is the first and least obvious question: Who is it that is learning these lessons? Who am I?"*

I am inviting you to explore that last crucial question, **"Who am I?"** from a few different perspectives. Stay awake and listen to your spirit for the

EXERCISE

Affirm to yourself out loud, "I claim my goodness, and my greatness, and I shine brilliantly."

answers. Even after you have gained clarity as you journey forward, keep asking. The reason that you keep asking is because you continue to evolve and therefore your answer might as well.

RE-BIRTHING THE SELF

As I've described, I began to wake up to my inner truths and deeper self when I moved to Hawaii in the early 1980s. That move started to open me to new ways of being in the world, and began forcing my bitter youth into a type of death and re-birth of its own. The God-fearing, holier-than-thou dogmatic teachings began to float away beyond the distant horizon far, far behind me. Moving to Hawaii from North Carolina was the greatest gift my mother ever gave me. There was a drastic change in the way people in Hawaii embraced cultural differences; it was night and day from how such differences were treated in the American South near the Cotton Belt. People there were less accepting of cultural diversity, often holding racist attitudes and treating one another harshly. In contrast, most neighborhoods and communities in Hawaii are of mixed ethnicities, and people are kind, culturally respectful, generous, open minded, and helpful. Locals say mahalo (thank you) often, even when they are driving! There is an authentic sense of community, of ohana (family), and connectedness with neighbors and haoles (foreigners or outsiders) not often found in other places. In my early years, I lived on the island of Oahu and later on the island of Maui. On both islands, I experienced being welcomed as part of families other than my own. With many people we remain close in spirit though I do not currently live in Hawaii.

That move to Hawaii began to open my eager eyes to new ways of living, though it wasn't until I was well into my thirties when I really woke up to my spirituality. I had to work through the sludge of my past and cut through the thickets of ego. But I did take with me, and keep with me, the essence of the Aloha Spirit (friendly attitude) that is powerful, graceful, and naturally good. There were quite a few times when I needed to re-acquaint myself with it, but it was always available. As I was learning to embrace the kindness and openness of my new home, I was also unlearning my rigid and closed thinking.

"The early morning breeze
has secrets to tell, do not
go back to sleep."
—*Rumi*

Coming to know the Aloha Spirit as a way of life helped me wake up to my divinity and to infinity.

Everyone who opens themselves to having a spirit-filled life will have their own awakening in their own unique ways. Can you think of ways you might be awakening to your soul or spirit at this time? Have you experienced any type of your own re-birthing? What parts of you might you want to re-birth now?

Native Hawaiians believe that healing and health comes from within. The following quote from Bula Logan, an herbalist from Oahu (appearing in a book titled *A Little Book of Aloha: Spirit of Healing*), represents this concept:

"Aloha has to begin with self. You have to love yourself.

You have to want to heal yourself.

Any aspect of dis-ease is a lack of aloha.

Aloha includes all the things aloha means,

there is all the respect. When you have respect you start to heal.

When you have lokahi (peace or unity) you start to heal.

The answer is when you look inside yourself—

do you feel good about yourself,

are you secure of who you are,

are you aware you created everything you wanted to create?"

NOTICING THOUGHTS

I have learned that we all have our own healing work to do, to wake up to our own Aloha Spirit. So how do you start? **You begin to awaken when you notice your thoughts.** The practice of noticing thoughts, your internal mental dialogue, will help you begin to see with new eyes and to increase your self-worth. This work is about a shift in perception. You are being asked to examine the voice in your head, to observe it, and to be okay with not knowing the outcomes of events and situations. Your mental patterns will become obvious, and you will learn to take a step back so you can view your thinking objectively. You eventually realize that the real you is the noticer, the observer, and the presence behind all of the noise. You are the witness of the voices of your mind. When it becomes a habit, this practice will serve as your ticket to **untie the knots** and **calm the jungle drums** of ego that keep you from living a flowering and fragrant life.

Thoughts give meaning to things, people, events, and situations. You give meaning to what you think you know. You give meaning to what you name to be true. You give meaning to what you think is real. Meanings are attached to suffering as well as to joy. Pain and suffering are real. No one can escape these aspects of being human, yet there are ways we might move beyond it or decrease the intensity or change the perception of the pain.

We all tend to associate meanings and feelings with pain. Think about any physical pain you've experienced. Do you recall how you described the pain? I have heard a number of people say, "My back hurts so bad it feels like it is breaking." Some people say, "It's killing me!"

I, too, have experienced severe back pain and sometimes said, "I don't know how I can go on like this! Why did I get this now? I can't take it! I don't deserve this!" But I always did go on, even with the pain. I found ways to reduce the pain, and I tried new things that helped. Eventually, with a diligent mindful practice, I learned to be gentle with myself about pain and decreased the drama and stress I had surrounded it with. I learned to **notice "sensations"** in my body versus naming them as pain. I began shifting my thoughts and words about the pain so I now say, "Hello, bodily sensation. Here you are. So I am going to calmly note your presence, and I am going to breathe into you. I am **curious** about what you might be here to teach me. I am going to lovingly nurture you and then release you."

What types of things do you tell yourself about pains? Think about it, then consider how true those meanings and feelings really are and how you might be able to shift your thoughts about dealing with them. Try to become more aware of pain instead of reacting to it. See it. Understand it. Realize its reason for arising. Do not judge it. Be with it.

Meanings and feelings are important, but they are not "real" in the true sense of the word—they are concepts in your mind that you attach to your pain and suffering. **Pain and abuse are indeed real, but you**

can control the meaning and the feeling you attach to it. I want to help you transcend, not deny, suffering. May you eventually celebrate possibility even in the dark.

The Buddhist teacher and author, James Baraz, writes about choices in his book *Awakening Joy*. Baraz says we have choices in terms of how we deal with suffering. He says we could:

1.   Avoid or deny.

2.   Resist and grow bitter.

3.   Endure it and resign yourself to your bad luck.

4.   Discern that there is another way that opens you to wisdom and to life itself.

Baraz goes on to say, "Our life circumstances change all the time. To a great degree, how much joy we have in our lives is determined not by what is happening, but how we respond to it."

What Baraz is getting at is that you can dissolve the negative meanings you attach to things to help stop the suffering or at least to experience far less of it. This is not about having a "spiritual bypass," as it's called. This process of noticing thoughts helps you to get through the issues that life puts before you as you become more focused on your present moments and how you might respond to them with less stress and **greater peace.**

Later on I will encourage you to go deeper into your experiences by examining your feelings and the full spectrum of your pain and suffering. I will ask you to complete some exercises to give you more of the flavor of this. I am aiming to help you get to a place where you can take the good and the bad together—to be able to detoxify the bad, negative, and hurtful experiences, and allow yourself to make meaning out of them in a way that supports your psychological well-being and your overall health and life.

SHIFTING THOUGHTS

Here is an example of shifting thoughts. When Valerie Harper (you might remember her from the television show "Rhoda") was diagnosed with terminal brain cancer, she was in touch with a larger perspective. Her response was, "Well, we are all terminal." Think about it for a few moments. It is true that **we are all on a trajectory towards aging, decline, and death**. You also have **choices** about how you react to such changes, and how to prepare for them. Therefore, how you prepare and think about dying can guide you to living more consciously, making better choices **now.**

Pause here to note that considering one's own mortality may not be an easy thing to do. And sometimes being lovingly direct about this fact of life is the best way to face it. As you proceed, stop at any time to take a few deep breaths. Acknowledge that your deep inner work requires this level of inquiry. This is an immensely profound practice, yet it has so much peace to offer you. I gently urge you to shift any fearful thoughts to peaceful thoughts as you continue.

Through some tough life lessons, I have learned the value of understanding impermanence and not to wait until I get older to learn how to grieve. Life is teaching us about loss and love. We lose people, dreams, physical strength, work, homes, careers, relationships, and health. We only grieve for what we love. It is important to allow the process of grief. It is essential to surrender to the emotional pain. I like to use the metaphor of the spiral in a nautilus shell—we release, and the pain comes back on deeper levels; the process coils through periods of intense feelings. We must be brave enough to go in, so we can come out stronger, wiser, and more connected to all of life. We can learn to be patient with the healing process of grief and not turn away from it or become stoic about it. Embracing our mortality means knowing that love is stronger than death. Our souls remain.

Remember at any time you can try to focus on positive mental states, which could help you shift behaviors and adjust how you experience life. It may take some practice, but with time I am confident you will get the hang of it. There are quite a few ways to **shift your thought processes** and I will show you how as we continue.

In my early days as a Clinical Social Worker I worked with a number of survivors of domestic violence at the District Attorney's Office in New Orleans, Louisiana. I observed that when clients began to shift from a "victimization" mentality to one of "survivor," they became empowered to start making safety plans (pre-conceived plans to escape abusive situations). After this shift some were more likely to realize that getting out of the abusive situation for good was a viable option.

One woman became empowered when she named her primary reason for staying "victimized." She told me, "It's because I can't read." She was a lovely woman, with a big heart and seven kids to feed. She was scared to leave an extremely abusive relationship in part because she felt she had no resources as a result of not being able to read. We made great progress together when she was able to tell me about the personal insecurity she had been harboring with great shame. When she revealed the illiteracy, I helped her find a free reading program—and a creative solution to participate in the classes without the perpetrator finding out. A few months later, she returned to my office beaming with hope because now she could read basic sentences. Together we evolved her "safety plan" into a "leaving the abuser plan." That wasn't the only issue I helped her work through—domestic violence is a complex and sensitive matter. There were layers of work that helped this client change her way of perceiving herself and her options.

Baraz writes, "There is a story that tells of the Buddha on his quest to find true happiness in a world full of suffering. His journey led him to conclude the more we face the fact that suffering is a part of life, the greater the possibility of experiencing the happiness of a mind liberated from stress. When he was asked about the essence of his teaching, the Buddha replied, 'I teach about suffering and the end of suffering.'"

By recognizing your thoughts, you will notice the subtle, and not so subtle, messages you tell yourself. Even if you have dark thoughts, or are in deep grief, or have suffered from physical abuse, there are important messages you can begin to hear or patterns you may begin to notice. The main point in this chapter is to begin to **slow down enough to hear the thoughts**.

Noticing your thoughts helps you pause more and drink in the silence of life so you can get focused for healthier and more fulfilling living. By noticing thoughts you can shift more readily to **compassionate, peaceful,**

EXERCISE

Take a moment to reflect on the thoughts coming up for you right now. Write these down in your journal.

prosperous, generous and similar ways of being in the world. I will also be inviting you to use your breathing to help you become more present to your thoughts. For now, you are being invited to simply begin to notice your thoughts. Go ahead and take this practice of noticing your thoughts one step further with the exercise.

THE MIND AS SPIRITUAL ESTATE

So often we go around living reactively and robotically, thinking about the way other people do things, wondering, "How can I be more like them or get what they have?" And what we really want to do is to become consciously aware of what is swirling around in our own minds so we can eventually get a grip on ourselves.

Your mind is a spiritual estate. You have access to unlimited creativity, joy, health, happiness, compassion, love, and abundance. Within you resides a bottomless well of **authentic, intuitive, and spiritual power.** You can draw from it any time by shifting your thoughts from the physical plane to the spiritual. Eventually you can build awareness within yourself, such that you have less and less dramatic reaction to all of life and more calm response. You become a **keen observer** of all your thoughts, thus imparting loving energy and setting an example for others. In grasping these concepts, you begin to **make choices that sing to your soul.**

> ### EXERCISE
>
>
>
> Answer the following questions in your journal.
>
> 1. How has my thinking let the expectations of others guide my life?
>
> 2. What thoughts have I had lately about comparing myself to others?
>
> 3. What kinds of messages have I been telling myself, in terms of wanting material things or desiring a life like someone else's?

Before I go on, I want to say that by no means do I think you can cure pain and suffering just by thinking positive thoughts. Dr. Bruce Lipton, Ph.D., teaches in his book *The Biology of Belief* the importance of managing both the conscious parts of the mind (thoughts, identity, source, spirit, creative mind) and subconscious parts (a repository of stimulus-response tapes derived from instincts and habitual learned experiences). Lipton says,

> *"The profoundly important fact is that disempowering programs in the subconscious mind can be quickly rewritten."*

Dr. Lipton also suggests using techniques such as hypnotherapy, affirmations, body-centered therapies, and a large number of modalities collectively referred to as "energy psychology." We will also be using affirmations and guided imagery to help you manage your mind and reach your goals.

As a Unity Prayer Chaplain, I learned some basic principles that guided me to further help people with their states of mind. Here is one:

> *"Human beings create their experiences by the activity of their thinking. Everything in the manifest realm has its beginning in thought. Thoughts in mind produce after their kind."*

Take a few moments to re-read that principle and see if it resonates with you.

Unity publishes a world-wide prayer booklet titled *Daily Word*. I have been reading this daily for over seven years. This "little booklet" is a powerful healing tool. One of my all time favorite daily messages on the topic of thoughts, feelings, and healing is as follows:

> *"Aware that my body responds to my thoughts and feelings, I release any worries I may have about health and healing. Instead, I focus my attention on the life of God within me. There is no disease or imperfection in God. I recognize this truth and celebrate the health and wholeness of my body temple. I thank my cells for their continuous renewal that provides my organs and tissues with new life. I marvel at the energy of God pulsing through my arteries. I am grateful that every system in my body is working to maintain balance and health. As I think about the many ways my body— God's perfect creation—serves me, my heart fills with gratitude."*

EXERCISE

Reflect for a moment on the above Unity *Daily Word* message. Do you sense the healing power in affirming those words? Take the time to consider which parts of the passage resonate most with you.

MINDFULNESS

Noticing thoughts is also known as "mindfulness," which is a scientifically proven method for coping and healing. The website, Mindfullivingprograms.com, provides useful approaches to understanding more about mindfulness. There one learns,

> *"Mindfulness meditation is moment-to-moment awareness.*
> *It is being fully awake. It involves being here for the*
> *moments of our lives, without striving or judging."*

Stillness and meditation practices can help you to learn to watch your thoughts and slow down your reactions to life's stressors. Practicing these techniques offers you a way **out of the endless spinning of your thoughts and fears.** With mindfulness you touch universality and timelessness. You live more in the present.

Dr. Jon Kabat-Zinn developed the Mindfulness Based Stress Reduction (MBSR) program at the University of Massachusetts Medical Center. The website talks about this program:

> *"Since its inception, MBSR has evolved into a common*
> *form of complementary medicine addressing a variety*
> *of health problems. The National Institutes of Health's*
> *National Center for Complementary and Alternative*
> *Medicine has provided a number of grants to research*
> *the efficacy of the MBSR program in promoting healing.*
> *Completed studies have found that pain-related drug*
> *utilization was decreased, and activity levels and feelings*
> *of self-esteem increased, for a majority of participants."*

The website goes on to say,

> *"Two decades of published research indicates that the*
> *majority of people who complete the MBSR Program report*
> *lasting decreases in physical and psychological symptoms."*

The MBSR studies report the following:

- Dramatic reductions in pain levels and an enhanced ability to cope with pain that may not go away

- Dramatic decreases in anxiety, depression, hostility, and the tendency to realize physical manifestations of psychological states

- More effective skills in managing stress

- An increased ability to relax

- Greater energy and enthusiasm for life

- Improved self-esteem

- An ability to cope more effectively with both short and long-term stressful situations.

A 2013 article titled "Depression-Proof Yourself" from *Spirituality and Health* magazine demonstrates the power of thinking patterns and making choices. Author Claudia Pinto writes:

> *"As it turns out, misery really does love company.*
> *A recent University of Notre Dame study of 103 pairs*
> *of roommates found that negative thinking patterns can*
> *be passed from person to person, just like the flu."*

Pinto goes on to say,

> *"'Cognitive vulnerability'—the mind-set that you're*
> *at fault for stressful life events and unable to change*
> *them—is particularly catching, increasing the symptoms*
> *of depression in others even six months later."*

The article further suggests that you can practice **compassion** for those in despair, practice **non-attachment** by observing with **curiosity** to limit exposure, and keep in mind that happiness is contagious, too. Lastly, Pinto states,

> *"We are all energetic beings. We become what we eat, what*
> *we watch, the people we surround ourselves with."*

There is sufficient evidence showing how powerful these techniques can be. Your practice can help you manage your mind so you can manage your choices and behaviors, and therefore your life.

Although some of the exercises in this book may be challenging, they will help you unlearn your previous habits and complicated ways of living and thinking. They can also aid you in letting go of the false identities society has imposed upon you—an identity of suffering and victimization and of not knowing yourself from a naturally loving perspective.

You can begin stepping into a **spiritual framework for living a more mindful, heart-centered, open, flexible, and passionate life.** Much like the ʻaina (land) of Hawaii itself, I hope you wake up to know the landscapes of you, the dark and light valleys of your personality, the molten hotness of your passions, and the warmth and coolness of all of your emotions, the expansive sea of your thoughts, the miraculous nature of your body temple, and the ancient depths of your soul. **Say, "aloha" (welcome) to the unfolding of the spirit and authentic power within you.**

As your guide, I encourage you to wake up to your transcendent self by reminding you to change your manaʻo (mind) and to shift your attitudes. I want you to be in the place where you know your thoughts and related actions, a place from which you can create your life the way you want it to be. I will be gently inviting you to try more exercises and nudging you to go deeper as

EXERCISE

For one week, notice your thoughts and what comes up for you emotionally. Whatever you are doing—driving, working, watching television, listening to a friend, or observing a sunset, be with your thoughts and notice how your feelings emerge with your thoughts; notice too your reactions such as wanting to cut someone off, or to give advice, or if your mind wanders. Take time to journal about your experience.

we progress through each chapter. As long as you hold an open mind and an open heart, and are willing to try new things, this book can change your life. For some of you, your life will change by leaps and bounds. For others, you may experience gentle shifts. All of this is perfect. **Be kind to yourself** wherever you are in this journey and with each step you take.

In your noticing-thoughts practice, you might recognize that instead of fully listening to others you are forming judgments and not being a heart-centered presence. You might be forming your opinion before they have even completed a sentence. You might be starting to think of your story to share on the same subject before they have fully shared their story. Then you may interrupt them to share your story or to give them an idea or suggestion. Try to listen more, to both your inner thoughts and to others. See if you can let interrupting or negative thoughts glide by in your mind, while you try to stay positively focused on the present moment. Try to really listen and get yourself out of the way. Try not to respond to others by offering your unsolicited opinions, suggestions, or ideas. Again, just listen, and note what choppy or bouncy thoughts might be going through your mind. Returning to yourself in the present moment allows you to keep in touch with the peace that is there.

As you keep practicing you will see that true happiness derives from being fully conscious in present moments—aware of your deeper connection to people and to everything else in the universe.

If you are observing your thoughts about yourself, take note of the words you use to describe yourself. Notice if you put yourself down or call yourself negative names. As you observe nature, take note of how your mind wanders to other things, perhaps to a work or family issue. The goal here is to try to **be as present as you can be—to what is—without judging, ridiculing, or getting off track.** Doing this exercise is very important to what comes next in the book so please take the time to sit back and befriend your thoughts.

"As he thinketh within himself, so is he."
—*Prov.23:7*

CHAPTER 5: SUNSHINE

Try to observe a sunrise before you contemplate and practice the waking up exercises in this chapter. By **pausing to reflect with nature,** you will be more centered, calm, and aware of your thoughts and feelings. In this chapter I help you see that directly focusing on the inevitability of change and loss helps you to be more buoyant with life. You will be asked to work through some challenging questions, to get comfortable with the idea that you can **live your life as if you were dying.**

Embracing the fact that death is a part of life is an essential part of opening to living fully. Can you see how you are like the sunrise, the sunshine, and the sunset? You die every day, and rise again the next. You begin, again, and again, and again. Every day is a new day to practice being just a little better than you were yesterday and to **awaken to the light within.**

DEATH AND LIFE

Borrowing from James Baraz once again, he tells us that The Buddha advised his followers to contemplate four truths:

1. This body will grow old; I am not beyond aging.

2. This body will become sick; I am not beyond sickness.

3. This body will die; I am not beyond death.

4. Everything near and dear to me will become separate from me.

"A realistic acceptance of death
is healthy, because it stimulates
a greater appreciation of
the value of our lives."
—*The Dalai Lama*

CULTURAL IMPACTS ON DEATH, FEARS, IDENTITY, GRIEF, AND LIFE

We begin at the end, so to speak…dying in American culture is usually viewed as a dark and fearful concept, one we do not have to accept. Think about it: when someone physically dies, we often ask, "How can this be so?" Yet we all know that dying is a natural part of life. One reason is that we are taught to live from fear. We are taught to fear death, and therefore we end up fearing life!

Think of how much society and culture imbeds fear into your thinking. Fear teaches you to think and act desperately in life and therefore to get what you want at all costs, even hurting or manipulating others to get your needs met, either blatantly or subtly. This produces a constant state of stress, anticipated grief, living in fear of your own death or that of others, and in fear of not having enough of anything. As you've grown, you probably have unlearned a lot of this; yet like most of us, you can un-do this even more.

The issue is that people get attached to ideas, ownership, relationships, other people, land, things. They also get stuck in their fears and in their grieving process even before they are actually dying or losing anything. Society has people falsely believing that they need branded products to make them feel good, healthy, perfect, alive, and loved. This is a phony identity, of course. This conditioning keeps people purchasing, acquiring debt, getting more of everything, over identifying with the physical body, material goods, and status. What happens is they **are lost and off course** which is not fully living. I've been in over my head with this sense of being adrift also, and I am confident that we all have been to one degree or another. This is the real bottom line here: What people are actually grieving is the **loss of their genuine identity**—their spiritual essence and their divine nature, and not all the material goods in the world will ever bring anyone authentic happiness.

Let me be clear about this: My point is not that material goods are all bad. Living a spiritual life does not mean one needs to get rid of all possessions. We obviously need certain physical things, and it feels good to give and receive gifts. It is our over-identification with things, the quantity of things, and the spending beyond our means that get us in trouble. When things begin to define us, that, my friend, is called unconscious, careless living. It is time to get real

"Love is eternal so death need
not be viewed as fearful."
—*Gerald Jampolsky, M.D.*

about your level of unawareness and your true need, which is **LOVE**. This is true for **all of us. We all need to learn to love ourselves in healthy ways.**

Consider this: Grief can be seen as the other side of love. Honestly ask yourself, **"Is there any part of me that is grieving my loving nature?"** As you continue to work through these chapters you might actually start to experience some or all of the stages of grief as you shed your old identity, old patterns, and old energy. The stages of grief are: denial, anger, bargaining, depression, and acceptance. Everyone grieves differently. Any or all of these stages are fine. Just note them, be with them, and move through them as best as you can.

Grief invites you into the mystery of life, and it is the wise ones who know that even with death (of any type) one can still choose peace and happiness. Death is life's greatest teacher. It teaches you about loss and can show you how to **appreciate and love more deeply**, open yourself to new ideas, detach from unhealthy attachments, open up to new perspectives, and create new energy.

Grief can be viewed as sacred energy and an opportunity for growing, expanding, and evolving. In grief and loss, if managed well, one essentially learns to accept significant change and move into new ways of living. With the death of a relationship, for example, the energy has changed.

To show you what I mean, think of someone going through a divorce or break up. Often there are broken hearts or anger or sadness. The healthy way through the change is to feel the feelings, grieve the loss, get support, accept the changes, and move on. Timelines vary from person to person of course. The crisis stage of grief will pass. Usually the person will end up feeling lighter and happier, ultimately finding some type of gift in the loss. Although deep feelings don't disappear completely, one can continue to hold great love for a person but recognize that accepting, releasing, and letting go is the healthier choice. A sense of grief may remain, but life will look and feel very different.

They have moved with and through the changes. As a result their energy will lighten up. They hold a positive attitude despite the changes. They have found a way to cope, function, learn, and let go. Yet if someone stays stuck in a deep sadness that evolves into a severe depression, they can become debilitated and afflicted with low energy. Very sadly some become suicidal. They may carry extreme heaviness everywhere they go, and they need professional help.

Most of us have been around someone or a group of people and said to ourselves, "Their energy is so negative, I can't be around them anymore." This typically includes the chronic complainers, the gossipers, the whiners, and those with "poor me" stories. Do you see how there is a difference in energy between, on the one hand, someone who can express a disappointment about a change but not be overcome by it or steeped in it and, on the other, someone who is stuck in a story of disappointment about change day after day?

So you get to choose how to deal with change and therefore your energy level. In general this also predicts how you might deal with loss or with change of any kind. If you cannot handle changes at work very well, then you are not likely to handle changes at home and vice versa. How you deal with change will determine the kind of energy you carry around with you day after day and wherever you go. Have you ever asked yourself, "What kind of energy do I normally embrace? What kind of energy do I emit on a daily basis? What kind of energy do I really want to embody?" Am I choosing negative or positive energy?

Consider this: If you know that love is the essence of all there is, then there really would be no separation, and therefore no real birth or death, of anything. Physically there will be a separation, but spiritually there will not be. Again what occurs is a shift in energy. Keep your heart open as you proceed.

I invite you to state the following out loud to yourself, and note your feelings:

1. From deep within myself I know that nothing external in life is secure, nothing physical ever lasts.

2. No matter how hard I may try, in the long run I cannot escape the devastating fact of death. Death is a destination that we all share.

3. An encounter with death can leave me changed decidedly for the better.

4. Connection to love can be my greatest life aspiration, even within the experience of death and dying.

5. Grief and loss are normal parts of the physical human experience, and it is healthy to move through the grief process.

6. I would not grieve if I didn't love.

7. In grief and loss, I do not have to attach myself to anyone or anything.

8. Life and death can be seen as shifts in energy and as miracles.

Again, consider this in terms of any sort of life and death. You might look back on a past unhealthy relationship and say to yourself, "I can see now that the divorce was a miracle. I would not have met my current wife who is my true soul mate if I had not divorced years ago. The death of that relationship allowed me to meet my new spouse whom I adore." One can even note that a physical death was a miracle such that the dying person no longer endures immense pain and suffering. I am using "miracle" here as a change in your own perception; thus, a miracle can be a change in thought. This will be explored a bit more as you read on.

EXERCISE

Take a moment to note your feelings and where any of the above statements might make you feel more free or uncomfortable. Examine where you might be closing your heart. There is nothing else to do at this point. Just note where you are with these ideas and try not to judge anything. Take a few deep breaths if you need to pause and reflect; write in your journal if you feel the urge to do so.

9. I can use the grieving process to heal from loss and as a way to love all of life more deeply.

10. Death is natural and inevitable but having a fear of death is not rational.

11. Love always remains.

12. I accept death as a part of life, and I am free to live my greatest life.

I really want to help you live your ho'oilina (legacy), to rise-n-shine—to wake up—to **live beyond your fears, including fear of death, and your fear of greatness,** so you can live at the highest energy frequencies available—**to begin living a fully self-actualized life.** Not living from your truth and keeping your light dim delays and cuts your dreams and goals—this is equal to spiritual suicide. Therefore, I want you to **stop waiting** for the right moment, resources, or time and **start creating** those moments by connecting with your inner light and the right resources. You have to choose how you think about life and what you do with your time day after day.

EXERCISE

Repeat the following out loud three times: "I say YES to my inner light and my whole life right now. I say YES to my happiness, to peace, to my dreams, to my potential, and to my unfolding future."

Some days will feel easier than others. But I am giving you the resources to help you keep yourself focused and strong, and to turn your pain and loss into **the greatness that you are.**

Not everyone will feel compelled to create "more" of their life or to change their purpose as there are ranges of need at any given time. Many people will feel they already have the resources they need. However, what I do know is that no matter one's level of awareness or current state of self-realization, we are all **evolving,** and therefore some sense of on-going practice is required to stay in the higher energy zones and to stay pono (balanced). I invite you to not resist but to persevere in your work with the practices. No matter where you are in your life on the actualization spectrum, I am confident you can embrace new ideas, change, loss, and pain while lovingly pushing yourself and harnessing your will to challenge yourself in new ways that **expand your consciousness and ways of living. Stay open. Keep your heart open.**

EXERCISE

Ponder each question below. They are designed to get you thinking about your legacy and your life purpose.

1. What does death mean to me?

2. What does life mean to me?

3. Am I willing to "die" to old ways of thinking?

"Though no one can go back
and make a brand new start,
anyone can start from now and
make a brand new ending."
—*Carl Bard*

Embora ninguem possa voltar
atras e fazer um novo comeco
Qualquer um pode comecar a
partir de agora e fazer um novo
fim

See if you can imagine the concept of dying as freeing yourself from pain, suffering, or (blank), you name it here. It is okay if you feel a little scared or unsure.
Just try to kalele (trust) in this process and be willing to stay open to new ideas.

No Coming, No Going

"This body is not me.
I am not caught in this body.
I am life without limit.
I have never been born and I never die.

"Look at the ocean and the sky filled with stars,
Manifestations from my wondrous true mind.

"Since beginningless time, I have always been free.
Birth and death are only doors through which we pass,
Sacred thresholds on our journey.
Birth and death are a game of hide-and-seek.

"So laugh with me,
Hold my hand,
let us say good-bye,
say good-bye to meet again.

"We meet today,
we will meet tomorrow,
we meet at the source in every moment,
we meet each other in all forms of life."

—Thich Nhat Hanh

Below is a relevant example of an epitaph (one's legacy statement).

"He died as he lived—Conscious of God,
Fearless of death, and at peace."

—Statement by the family on the death of George Harrison

LIFE HAS YOUR BACK

I will offer you the opportunity to write your legacy statement in subsequent chapters. The contemplating of this exercise beforehand is a part of your awakening and life-defining process. Just feel into your experience and continue to journal as things come up for you.

As you work through the chapters in Act I, you are beginning to dip your toes into the pool of your sacred life. I am helping you to get familiar with the tides and waves of life before I invite you to fully dive in. Give yourself some credit for consciously choosing to live a deeply powerful and awakened life. Honor the work you have completed by taking a **deep breath** in this divine moment. Take a few more if you need to.

OLA (LIFE)

You are the star in your ola! **Claim it, sing it, dance it, and know it.** It is your divine nature.

My friend on Oahu grows a gorgeous Stephanotis vine, with a white star-shaped flower, on her garden fence. The meaning of the Stephanotis plant is "marital happiness," and brides often use this flower in their wedding bouquets. Whether you are technically married or not, **my wish for you is that you marry yourself to your true purpose for being in the world—and that you take a vow to live it every single day.**

ONENESS WITH SOURCE

You are from the same Source that that makes the sun rise, causes the flowers to bloom, propels the waves, aligns the planets, and gives the stars their sparkle! If you **connect deeply with nature**

EXERCISE

Envision yourself floating on tranquil warm waters. You feel safe and held by gently rocking waves. Mother Nature has your back. You are surrendering and waking up to your true self.

EXERCISE

Envision that you are high in the air holding onto a trapeze bar, and as you begin to release it, you faithfully reach out to embrace the new one that you can clearly see is already headed your way. Cultivate a sense of trust as you continue to practice—you are building a trusting muscle.

EXERCISE

Journal about how you are the star in your own life, or how you want to be the star in your own life.

"Behold, I tell you a mystery: We shall not all sleep, but we shall all be changed, in a moment, in the twinkling of an eye, at the last trumpet. For the trumpet will sound, and the dead will be raised incorruptible, and we shall be changed."
—*1 Corinthians 15:52, NKJV*

in this way, you might find that a spiritual truth for you is that you are a child of the larger divine energetic Source of all that is. You have the ability to be at one with this Source, to understand it, and to live in alignment with it. And you must do the inner work to get yourself there. It may feel difficult, or it may feel rather effortless. That part is up to you. For me, I had to move through quite a bit of darkness to see the light. The next section explains how I did it and how you can as well.

RE-CHARTING THE COURSE

Re-charting your course will help you become at one with your Source. Here is the story of how I reset my course; I hope it serves as a little spark of inspiration for you.

I do not remember what took me to the hospital at age four, but my mother tells me that I suffered from colon polyps and needed emergency surgery. The doctors made a twelve-inch-long incision in my abdomen. Being on my deathbed at such an early age would later give me a deep appreciation for life. After the life-saving surgery, I was weak and marked with an enormous scar down the center of my very thin and fragile body as I tried to play with the other kids. I was different, and I knew it. But it would take me many years to understand the gifts I had been given. Like most of us, I was not able to articulate and express my gifts until much later in life. Back then there were two parts or aspects to my nature. One was an anxious and weak little girl while another part was creative, adventurous, and determined. As an only child, my circumstances forced me to be introspective at an early age and to question God and religion. I questioned the hypocrisy of the adults around me. I really think one of the greatest gifts of being an only child is how introspective one

EXERCISE

Take a thirty-minute mindful walk in nature and find yourself there, wherever you are. Try to make a connection with nature based on how you are currently feeling, or how you want to feel. Maybe you will find yourself in a sunrise, or a most unusual flower, a light filtering tree, a curious lady bug, a slow moving caterpillar, or as a fluttering butterfly. Perhaps you will find yourself in the warm ocean breeze. Or maybe you will appear as a soaring bird, as a snow covered mountain, as the scent of a gardenia, or as a rising lotus. Maybe you will find yourself in the misty air, in the pouring rain, in a mud puddle, as a pile of crunchy leaves, in a spider web, or in a grain of sand. After you walk, take some quiet time to journal your experience. If the elements prevent you from going outside, just imagine your adventure in your mind or view nature through a window.

can be. The observing nature, the forced creativity, the ease with being alone instill enormous strength and natural leadership.

Though I very much knew the love of my mother, I also felt alone, sad, and unsure much of the time. My mom was often working several jobs to put a roof over our heads. My father died when he was just twenty-one years old. As a young girl I remember thinking, "If there was a God, how could he take away a little girl's daddy?" This question would be in my mind well into my thirties. My father Thomas Willard Heckman's death certificate read, "Excessive Inebriation." He overdosed on alcohol. My young mother, only twenty-one years old at the time, raised her only daughter—me—the very best way she knew how.

During those early years the family around me struggled with alcoholism, depression, anxiety, and poverty. There were several early deaths of family members, and I mentioned earlier the loss of one of my best friends who died in 9-11, which caused more grieving. There were many times when I had to make my way through deep feelings of insecurity, loneliness, loss, fear, and struggle. I learned through these challenges that I could make choices, though of course I didn't always make the right ones. I kept trying and forged ahead to live a healthier and happier life thus re-charting my course multiple times.

We were poor and I was the oldest grandchild, an only child, and had few friends. There was a poverty consciousness all around me especially in those early days. My mother married and divorced twice and when she was single things got even tougher. We moved a lot. She worked long hours and when she was not working we would often be at family parties. Frequently the adults would be intoxicated, and I would retreat to my room. I watched television, read the latest magazine or a *Nancy Drew* mystery, or played Barbies alone. I often turned up my music and danced or had friends over and taught them dance routines. My favorite songs to dance to were "Monster Mash," "Splish Splash I Was Taking a Bath," "Brick House," and anything by Elvis Presley or on the *American Grafitti* soundtrack. Our family just loved Elvis. In fact, my

EXERCISE

Think of a time in your life where you turned a challenging situation or experience into an opportunity or a gift. Now write in your journal about that experience.

very first concert, around the age of six, was Elvis at the Greensboro Coliseum with my mom and my great aunt. I barely remember it. Around the age of eleven I started rocking out to Ozzy Osborne, AC/DC, and Joan Jett. Music helped to get me out of my head.

There were many other times I just needed to get out of the house. I felt so cooped up with the howling adults swilling their beers and hard liquor. I would visit friends and play board games, take a few tumbles on a trampoline, or unleash my curiosity in nature before returning to the cackling hyena adults who seemed so foreign to me. I swear I never listened to their jokes and the stories they told; I made an effort not to. But I couldn't shut out the crazy roaring laughter and cracking open of each beer can. Sometimes it took a lot to keep myself occupied but I did a pretty good job overall.

In my hours of solitude sometimes I would slowly devour fashion catalogues page by page and make pretend purchases in my mind. I did this with furniture and home goods catalogues as well. At times I would draw my dream home or visualize a fantasy world of living in New York and throwing open the penthouse windows on Park Avenue like Zsa Zsa Gabor did on the television show *Green Acres*. Over the years I am sure I drew over thousands of those fantasy homes—some elaborate and some quite simple. Later I realized the drawings often provided a better sense of the structure and foundation—the "true home"—that I wanted.

Once I ventured off too far and got lost in the woods. It took many hours for my mom and step dad to find me. Another time I climbed a tree too high and was scared to come down. My mom had to come up and get me. No one would call me an obstreperous child. I was the quiet one, winning blue ribbon awards in elementary school for "good citizenship." So I never really got into serious trouble as long as my mother knew where I was or who I was with. But left to my own devices, I decided I could make up or do almost anything as long as it was in line with being a "good, quiet Southern girl." Since my mom was often working and I was bored a lot, I had to entertain myself on my own. I tried to get my mom to do more with me but she was often overworked, tired, and resting.

At other times I felt lonely and sad. I worried about money. I often asked about the household finances but I quickly learned those were adult matters—and also that the adults did not know how to manage the finances. On more than one occasion my requests for basics like new school clothes were met with standard platitudes: "Remember, there are starving kids in Africa" and "Money doesn't grow on trees." Well, that always shut me up. I accepted such responses as well as I could and went about life the best way I knew how. I kept envisioning what my life would be like once I became an adult. I cannot tell you how much my imagination helped give me hope, conviction, and tenacity.

My first step dad made me a bike out of parts pieced together with a sparkley red banana seat. It was so cool, mostly because of the shiney silver tassles I just had to have added.

One Saturday I rode to my friend Rita's house. Unbeknownst to me her parents were out of town and her older siblings were having a party. I parked my bike in the front of the house as usual. I was very uncomfortable navigating my way through that house packed with loud, older kids and teens. After just a little while I told Rita that I wasn't feeling good and needed to leave. When I came out my precious bike was gone. I ran home crying and told my mother. She was livid. We immediately took off in her two-door, avocado-green Nova and scoured the neighborhood. It did not take long to find the culprit. We turned a corner and there it was, my bike turned upside down right smack dab in front of a house, with an older kid preparing to take the wheels off. I will never forget that day. My mom swerved the car into the driveway, ran right up to that guy, and with her southern accent declared, "That is my little girl's bike and we are taking it home right now. Shame on you! Shame on YOU!!" She grabbed my bike and put it in the trunk of the car. My mom, my hero. Her fierce love for me showed up like that on a number of occasions. In my heart I knew she would give me all the money in the world if she could. And if she could do that, then she could also spend all the time in the world with me. If she could. It also helped that she told me she loved me all of the time.

One summer I took myself to the local pool almost every day and I taught myself to swim. I observed others and I talked to others. Some adults would also give me pointers on diving or about pool safety since I was without adult supervision.

At one point my mom ensured that her little girl enrolled in a local dance studio in spite of its high cost to our spare budget. I am certain our financial situation is why I had sugar laden cereal for breakfast, lunch, and dinner most of the time. A more "balanced" meal was the occasional fried weenie (hot dog) and macaroni and cheese or macaroni and tomato soup. Our cupboards were pretty bare. There'd be a few cans of tuna, deviled ham (which I hated!), Spam, or Vienna sausages. In the fridge we had sliced cheese, bologna, butter, ketchup, maybe a head of iceberg lettuce, and either ranch dressing or Italian. There was almost always an unusual spread that my mom loved—something gray and shaped like a rectangle called "Liver Pudding." She would swipe it onto white bread with a shmear of mustard. I tried it once but it made me gag. The most flavorful meal to me was a fried bologna sandwich, which was extra special when my mom made it for me. On special holidays or Sundays we enjoyed pinto beans with cornbread, or baked chicken, and on rare occasion a steak with baked potato.

I was pretty frail and thin, but I very much enjoyed the dance classes which included tap, jazz and baton twirling with regular recitals. I ate that "pretty girl on stage with a cute costume in the spot light" stuff up! Finally, instead of retreating from adults, I was getting noticed for something good and fun and it felt wonderful. My mom took me to my classes and attended my recitals. The adults around me encouraged my dancing, and I would tap and twirl my way into their hearts for all of the smiles and applause—whether they were tipsy or not. I devised many dance routines, both in my mind and with friends. I even entered a few talent competitions and won the talent portion of a show tapping my way and singing to "Summer Lovin'" from the *Grease* soundtrack.

In Hawaii, around the 6th through 9th grades I continued with dance classes, met wonderful new friends and often hung out at their family homes watching movies, listening to music, and enjoying wholesome meals. This was also around the same time that my step-grandparents were taking us out to marvelous local restaurants. Hawaii nourished me in many ways.

I loved listening to and dancing to music from the 80s—R.E.M., Adam Ant, Boy George, Erasure, Oingo Boingo, The Smiths, and Depeche Mode were my favorite bands. When I entered high school I gave up dance and tried to focus on my classes, joining social groups and going to parties. One of the counselors told me, "You are a very resilient person, Melissa." Her words gave me strength. At the time I really needed to hear that, and the truth is that I've embodied it to this day—*I am a resilient person*. I so appreciated the positive spin on my then stressful life. I often wished I could save my mom from her struggles to keep us financially afloat, but I was mostly just trying to be a teenager and find my way in the world. Eventually I started to work so I could have money for nicer clothes. The first job I found was seasonal—selling Halloween costumes at a small retail shop. In the 10th grade I started part-time modeling, landing small time fashion shows, fashion catalogues, and a few local television ads. The money helped me get the clothes, shoes, and accessories I desired. The jobs and the finer clothes helped my self esteem. I also enjoyed treating my friends to local eateries.

My time at Kalaheo High School was fun and difficult for me. My mom and second step dad divorced, and she had to work several jobs. She was under enormous pressure to provide and survive. I was busy going to school, working part time, and trying to be a typical teenager. My friends and boyfriend meant so much to me. From those same friends I got the idea that to have a happy and meaningful life, you had to leave home and go to college. The difference for them was that their college would be paid for. Plus, they actually got to travel to tour their respective options. That seemed so lavish to me, but I was happy for them. Without any financial backing myself, I just knew I had to get to college—somehow. My mom's strong words about pursuing education were foundational. She researched how to obtain school loans and helped me complete the applications. At that time it was all that I knew for certain about my future. I paid for the college applications with money I earned from modeling.

I put myself through college and graduate school in order to consciously expand my mind and to increase my experience of the world. There was something in me that wanted more out of life, and I knew that going to college was a smart choice.

As an adult I have also entered therapy off and on when I felt I was lost or needing extra support. It has always gotten me back on course or affirmed that I was right where I needed to be. I also observed my friends with their more "normal" or functional families. I confided in friends often and they inspired me to reach higher and higher. I just kept trying new things and explorng new places, and I read more and more. I tried to be social even though it was often awkward for me.

My mom returned to North Carolina when I graduated from high school in Hawaii. At first that separation was dramatic. It was hard for my mom to cut the symbolic umbilical cord. I headed off to Colorado State University on a financial need based scholarship and made mostly poor grades. As a first generation college student, I simply did not know how to study at that level. After one year applying myself as best as I could and missing Hawaii, I was somewhat depressed and frustrated so I moved back to Hawaii and tried to make it on my own. Again I worked as a model and started teaching modeling classes while living in a tiny studio apartment in Lanikai. It did not take me long to realize I wanted a college education no matter what. I was also greatly missing my mother. So I returned to North Carolina to complete my undergraduate studies with government grants and student loans. I took some classes at a community college then transferred to the four year university. That was a very wise stepping stone. I became fully engrossed in my studies often taking twenty-one credits per semester at the university while working part time retail jobs. I became involved with every extra curricular group that was of interest to me. One of the most rewarding was the Women's Leadership Coalition. After a lot of dedication and hard work, I obtained my B.A. in Sociology.

It was great being back in North Carolina at that time, mostly because it meant being closer to my mom who was doing much better. I could see that she was making great strides in her life as well. All in all, it was a happy time.

Yet I wanted more. I wanted more education, and to leave North Carolina again. I moved to New Orleans and enrolled in graduate school at the esteemed Tulane University. After two intensive years of study, an enormous school loan, and a few Mardi Gras parades, a graduate degree was under my belt as well. It seemed like only moments after I'd received the diploma, I had it framed and then wrapped up for shipment to my new office in Hawaii. I couldn't get *home* fast enough.

I worked as a Psychiatric Social Worker for Maui county. That move was one of both immense freedom and challenge. I felt profoundly happy to be working for the local population, to be enveloped by the island air, and to dig my toes in the sand again. And how adventurous it was to explore a new island in Hawaii! Yet I faced serious financial challenges while earning a small income as a social worker and trying to pay off my previous school loan. This was a slap in the face after all of my hard work to get out of poverty. So I suffered serious financial set backs and entered a period of familiar struggle once again. I sought financial counsel and was advised over and over again, "You just need to make more money. You need more income. You need a lot more to pay your bills and meet your basic needs." I racked my brain, talked to a few trusted friends, told my mom how bad things were on the financial front, and I searched and searched mostly outwardly at that time for answers. My mom so desperately wanted to help me but she was financially strapped too since she had her own college loans to pay off. In truth I did not always handle my finances properly. But I was not focused on being frugal. Frugal felt too much like poverty at that time. Like many people trying to get a better life, we think the one and only way to get ahead is to get a college education and that alone will be enough. For me I do feel it was the right thing to do even though I was drowning in debt for a number of years afterwards. Since then I've learned a lot about finances, spending habits, and self-negating choices—including the fact that "scraping together" is a mentality that I never want to have again.

Since college was familiar and I felt smart enough—and also knowing I could easily obtain school loans—I made the decision to go back to school yet again to earn a doctorate degree with the intention to eventually make more money, like all the financial advisors told me to do. At the time this felt like the best way to enhance my current skill set and to set myself up to earn a better income.

In a very short amount of time I was accepted into a small private school in San Francisco and would embark upon a doctoral program in organizational psychology. I sold almost everything I owned, moved to San Francisco right away, and worked full time for a non-profit while enrolled part time in the doctoral program. With über high rents, another low paying social work job, and after two semesters of busting my butt and feeling huge stress, I began to think about all of the additional school loan debt that I was accruing and how far away that doctorate really was—at least six to eight more years. At the same time I had a few panic attacks about those rising loans, and I evaluated the classes I was taking. It became clear I needed to plan better and feel even deeper to see if this was the correct career plan for me. In all honestly the classes were not fulfilling me. I was also not enjoying the subject matter, the books, or even the mind set of the people around me. It would take a while to realize that I longed to help people as a social worker again and not as an organizational consultant.

But before returning to social work I needed to check out a few pending opportunities to see if I could increase my income doing something totally different. At one point I was a human resource manager for a large multinational hotel chain. Unfortunately I felt like I was starting at the bottom of the totem pole even though I had enormous skill and talent to share. Most unfortunately it also felt insanely competitive—a rather unfamiliar and unnatural working environment for a social worker. On another attempt I was a swatch fabric coordinator for a national retail chain and that also felt incongruent for me. I dabbled around with different non-profits and tried to keep an open mind.

Trying out the dating scene and meeting new friends were also a new aspect to my life at the time but the dating scene proved unfulfilling as well. I went through breakup after breakup. With my resilient mindset, however, I kept at it—all of it. I knew in my bones that I would get to a much more stable place with career, finances, and relationships.

When I look back to note the turningpoint in my life, I have to say it was a combination of a few things that came into my life. First, I started to practice yoga in 2005, which helped me slow down and become more centered. Then there was *the* book that I discovered in 2006 by Dr. Wayne Dyer titled, *Inspiration: Your Ultimate Calling.* Dr. Dyer's teaching put spirituality in context for me. His teaching led me to locate a Unity center in Berkeley and to the book *A Course in Miracles.* I soaked up all of the New Thought teachings in book after book. I met positive, loving, creative people who I truly enjoyed being around. I also read and studied the *Tao Te Ching* by Lao Tzu. I got focused and clear, finally. Things began to fall into place and everything shifted for the better. My stories throughout the upcoming pages will help reinforce the importance of living from a spiritual framework for you and hopefully help you set your life direction as well.

I eventually could look at all of the family challenges, deaths, losses and my own struggles, as a way to learn about life and re-chart my course. I fell down quite a bit but I kept getting up with anticipation of new horizons. This is what we all must do to get beyond the rough patches and tumultuous times. As I've deepened in my spiritual practices, life has gifted me with stablility in all aspects, and things just keep getting better. I can honestly tell you that I no longer struggle with life. I work for a thriving company. Finances are good. I am content. I am at peace. I love my work. I return to Hawaii regularly to see my Ohana (family) friends. I am optimistic about the opportunities before me. I also have a wonderful, loving partner. At the same time I definitely aim for more progress and success in all areas because I want to help make significant changes for others while I am still capable. Life keeps waking me up. It keeps me motivated, encouraged, and inspired to take myself to greater heights in service to others and for the evolution of our planet. Life has great meaning, and I am living my purpose.

FULL STEAM AHEAD

You can imagine how the experience of knocking on death's door gave me a sense of gratitude for my life and inspired me to make the most of it. My ability to face my own mortality, and to be there for others as they face death in a medical setting, has been tremendously helpful to move me forward. My interest in counseling about death and dying stems from my passion for life and living. But as I shared, I had to look at death very early on. As a result, I strongly believe that by doing this work, we all can move through life more fluidly.

On our own, grieving, and thrust into an uncertain future, my mom and I grew up together and eventually moved way beyond the difficulties of that earlier time. It was my mother's determination, her hard work, the high value she placed on education, her sense of adventure, and her resilience that shaped me into the woman I have become. I am so happy to report that over the years my extended family made great strides as well.

By doing my inner work and shifting my mind-set from "poverty, devastation, and loss" to "wealth of mind, gifts, and challenges," I would come to know all of the scars of my life as essential to living with greater meaning and putting the experiences and my inner strength to use serving others.

I am delighted to share that my mom and I graduated from college in the same year and became different types of teachers and published authors.

MANAGING CHANGE

I want to remind you that you choose how to handle both everyday stressors as well as the really stormy times. You are fully capable of managing the inevitable changes of life with grace and ease, at one with your Source. Pause here and decide for yourself if you can be a little, or a lot, better at this.

Give some thought to how you manage change in general. Consider times when you moved, left a

EXERCISE

Contemplate each of the following questions and write your answers in your journal.

1. How is my life like the ebb and flow of the tides?
2. Do I roll with the changes of my life?
3. Do I allow myself to grow and blossom with each challenge?
4. Do I fight change and create more stress, anxiety, drama, or even illness?
5. Do I hold on to issues of the past that plague me and rob me of my precious life energy?
6. Could a particular challenge turn out to help serve as my purpose in life?
7. What might that be?

job, got sick, graduated, got lost, ended a relationship, experienced the death of someone close or even a pet, lost something important, or needed to change your schedule suddenly. You get the idea. Think of any example that comes up for you, and just go with it. Be very **honest and real with yourself**, then journal your thoughts.

As you proceed with each chapter you are awakening to a new dawn, a new you. Perhaps you already feel a strong pull to change how you are living and how you are currently managing things.

"The two most important days in your life are the day you are born…and the day you find out why."
—*Mark Twain*

CHAPTER 6: TO BEGIN AGAIN

In this chapter, I invite you to take the legacy work a bit further to begin to shape your life's purpose in the context of your contribution to healing larger social ills. I will also help you work on your values.

Just as the receding tide leaves an imprint in the sand, so will you. You will leave an imprint on the hearts and minds of those around you. As I've indicated, thinking about your legacy (how you wish to be remembered at the end of your life) helps you to decide how to start living your heart's desire—today. The "end" I am referring to is the very end of your life, the moment after you take your last breath. Consider your legacy carefully because now is the time to **get serious about transformation on this planet—how you want to leave it and therefore how you want to live on it**. Respectfully I say to you that you must know who you are and why you are here, and live from that place if you desire to live with more peace, greater joy, and a sustainable planet.

HEALING THE BODY OF THE WORLD

Our planet is suffering; too many of our brothers and sisters are suffering. I don't have to name more than a few issues to get the point across: poverty, addictions, mental illness, homelessness, the environment, obesity, genetically modified foods, nuclear accidents, cancer.

I believe we all must recognize that we are part of the larger body of the world, one organism. Every part affects the whole, just as a sick or healthy cell in the body affects the overall functioning of the body system. What we do or do not do matters not just for ourselves, but for our families and communities. If we are living our lives consciously, it matters. If we are living our lives on autopilot, lost, wandering, worried, fearful, or trying to get ahead of others—trying to

"If one wants to die peacefully, one must begin helping oneself long before the time to die has come."
—*Swami Muktananda*

win at all costs—**it matters.** The real bottom line is that **values** expressed by our **choices** matter on both an individual and a larger scale. Negative thoughts, words, and actions matter, and they will leave negative or fearful footprints for future generations. Positive thoughts, words, and actions will leave loving imprints and a more peaceful world.

The larger organism of life is affected by you. You can choose to create healthier energy by being your very best self, or you can choose to strengthen the darker, negative energies that serve no one and only continue to create more ego-based behavior patterns, wars, destruction, and suffering. By being your own "best self" I am not referring to attaining perfection. I am suggesting that you take full **responsibility** for your life in the context of understanding **how** your life impacts others.

DEATHBED FEARS

When I was a Medical Social Worker in an Intensive Care Unit, I saw countless fearful faces at the bedside of many people. I have witnessed suffering groans from patients and their loved ones. One day I was doing my rounds at the hospital and it occurred to me that I had visited at the bedside of several patients who told me stories of having lost hope in life many years before. There were stories of unresolved family feuds and stories of feeling alone and bitter. There were stories of holding grudges. Many of these people felt frightened about dying. This sudden realization that people were dying in fear shook me to the core.

My continued practice working with patients who are chronically ill often gives me great pause about

EXERCISE

Answer the following questions:

1. Do I feel I contribute to the whole of life with my daily choices?

2. How might my daily choices affect not only my family but my community and society as a whole?

3. Do I want to be remembered for my contributions to my family and to all of life?

EXERCISE

Ask yourself the following questions and then journal your thoughts.

1. If I died today, would I have any regrets? What would they be?

2. If I knew I was going to die within the year, what MUST I do today, for myself, my family, my neighbors, my community, for the world?

3. To whom do I need to say "I love you" more frequently? Now, go and do it. Make calls, set a date, send a card, write a letter, mark it in the sand, draw it, paint it, sing it, or send an email. Even a text will do!

how I am living my life. In my career, I've realized that Western Medicine could do so much more for patients earlier on. So I started to ask chronically ill patients in the clinic setting about their legacy. At the same time I began to tie in their legacy and purpose with their health care treatment goals. Patients have conveyed to me that they are highly appreciative of this part of the discussion. I enjoyed giving these types of soulful "prescriptions" in many types of settings and I honestly believe **one of the best types of "medicine" we can give ourselves is to find, know, and live our life purpose**.

With these exercises and your insights from journaling and reflection, you have an opportunity to give yourself a healing tonic. You can heal—your body, your mind, and your soul. You can begin again, to assess where you are with the concepts of dying and living as well as to clarify your life purpose so you **do not go to your deathbed wishing you had done it all differently,** or that you did your part to leave the planet a better place for your children or grand children.

These exercises might appear to be focused on dying, but they are actually designed to help you start living from a deeply loving space and to do important things today, while you are living. I am taking you deep as you analyze "the end" because I want you to be fully prepared to dive into the middle chapters. If nothing comes up for you with regard to the last exercise, that is fine. You will have another opportunity to revisit the legacy work later on, and to refine your answers. Right now just allow the process to flow as it needs to, without concern for the outcome. Continue to feel through each exercise and at least try them. Go as far as you can with each one.

EXERCISE

Ask yourself the following questions then write about your thoughts in your journal. Consider these as a draft of what you will be asked to complete in later chapters.

1. What kind of mark do I want to leave in the world?

2. What do I want my ho'oilina (legacy) to be?

3. What might my true life purpose be?

EPITAPH

An epitaph is an inscription on a gravestone. Often it reads as a short description of how the deceased would like to be remembered or how the family remembers the deceased. I invite students in my coaching workshops to consider how they might want their epitaph to read, and I ask them to draft a few lines. Although it is a challenging exercise for many, afterwards they tell me how thought provoking and important it is. Below is one example of an epitaph from a highly regarded psychiatrist:

ELISABETH KÜBLER ROSS, MD

Loving Mother and Grandmother
Compassionate friend, teacher, & student

Graduated to "dance in the galaxies"
On August 24, 2004
"WE'LL BE LOVING YOU ALWAYS"

LIFE PLANNING CHALLENGE

The following suggested exercises are for those who feel they are ready to make more end of life plans. These are optional exercises you can do any time.

1. Ask your medical doctor about completing your Advanced Directive paperwork. This paperwork forces you to think about end of life issues such as who you would want to make medical decisions on your behalf should you not be able to do so for yourself. This includes considering if you would want cardiopulmonary resuscitation, feeding tubes, and breathing ventilation machines.

2. Research the location of where you might want your memorial service held, the type of casket you want, or where you would be cremated.

EXERCISE

If you feel ready, write out an outline, or a draft, of your epitaph. Optionally, you could also write out a draft of your funeral ceremony (or your celebration of life). Consider the type of music you want, poems for people to read, and any other creative ideas that come to mind. Consider what message you would want to leave for your kids, spouse, partner, parents, friends, siblings, or others such as mentors, teachers, and advisors, people who have inspired you or helped you in some significant way. Remember that this is just an outline or draft of your ideas for now. Take a few deep breaths as needed and stop writing when it feels right. The following exercise on values might help you craft this as well. Come back if you need to.

"I don't want my heritage
of joy to die."
—*Pablo Neruda*

VALUES

I turn now to ask you to think about what you value most in life. By exploring and naming the values you hold most dear, you will be able to crystallize your vision of your legacy and life purpose later on. Be gentle with yourself and really hone in on how far you are willing to go with this exercise. Then honor yourself. Just do what feels comfortable to you at this time.

The goal here is to be clear about what you value so you will begin living in alignment with your deepest positive desires. Remember to be patient with yourself. Come back to this exercise in a few days if you need to.

Wherever you are on your journey right now is perfect. Accept that getting clear is not an overnight process. Your discernment of these matters will become more and more vivid as you proceed. If you have defined your legacy and values already, allow this process to refine your work or help you open to new insights.

I have written and refined my legacy and values a few times over the years, and it is freeing to continue having new ideas and observations about it.

> ## EXERCISE
>
>
>
> List your values in your journal. Consider what really matters to you, such as creativity, peace, God, family, relationships, integrity, a hobby, laughter, nature, and a sport. The list can be as long as you want it to be. Then, circle three of your favorites. They should be the ones that resonate most deeply as a true part of who you are. Do not ask, "What would my parents, spouse, or siblings want me to say?" Let go of outside influences, and simply listen to what your inner voice is saying. After you have circled your top three, then choose the one that most resonates with you. Keep this value in your mind as you proceed and are asked to complete the remaining exercises.

Because we are **evolving beings**, it makes sense that our ideas and ways of living will evolve too. I find this element of change in life exciting! We get to change! What an opportunity. Think of how boring things would be if nothing ever changed.

Having taken a look at your life legacy and values, take a moment to appreciate yourself for participating in this clarifying process. Reflect on what you wrote and give yourself permission to put it away for now. You will be able to refine these concepts later.

RE-BIRTHING

The reason I have an on-going love affair with Hawaii is that the land and its Aloha Spirit helped to re-birth me. Growing up there opened my mind and heart and began to help clarify my purpose in the world.

There are many locations in the 'aina (land) that help me to remember where I came from and, more importantly, where I am and where I am going in life.

In addition to Lanikai, my favorite spots for reflection include the long strand of Kailua's white sand beach stretching from the northern tip of the military base to the southern end of Lanikai and Keawakapu beach on Maui's southwest side, with its perfect sunset views that offer the islands of Kahoolawe, Molokini, and Lanai as spectacular backdrops. At Lanikai it is all about the sunrise, and at Keawakapu it is all about the sunset. These two places remind me to surrender my light to the world and that **each day is a new day, to clarify, and begin again**.

What locations inspire you? How does nature get you to think differently about your life? What song can become your new life theme song? What can be "born again" in you?

"That's how we live, Always
Saying good-bye."
—*Rilke, 8th Duino Elegy*

AND YET...

"How does an essence of the
world leave the world? How
does wetness leave the water?
Don't even try. You
are here to stay."
—*Rumi*

CHAPTER 7: LIFE REVIEW

Now you will embark on a hua'kah'i (journey) to clarify important domains of your life. This next exercise helps to clarify where your strengths are and where you need to focus for change. Once you rate your domains, you will have an opportunity to create a simple structured plan for self improvement. You will also be provided a simple formula for attaining your goals.

Remember, **you do not need fixing in a spiritual sense.** In the spiritual realm you are already perfect in the eyes of the divine. So, perhaps you can see this as more of a fine tuning and an opportunity to tap more deeply into your divine purpose for living on the physical plane.

EXERCISE

Please complete the following brief assessment to rate your life domains. Circle the number that feels most correct for where you are in each area of life. This is to lead you towards clarity about the main areas of your life, what you are doing well and those areas that you need to work on. Don't over think this. Try to choose the first response that comes to your mind. There are no "right" or "wrong" answers.

DOMAIN SCALE (CURRENT DEGREE OF SATISFACTION)

Spirituality	(needs serious work)	1 2 3 4 5 6 7 8 9 10	(fully satisfied)
Family	(needs serious work)	1 2 3 4 5 6 7 8 9 10	(fully satisfied)
Career/Work	(needs serious work)	1 2 3 4 5 6 7 8 9 10	(fully satisfied)
Overall Health	(needs serious work)	1 2 3 4 5 6 7 8 9 10	(fully satisfied)
Diet/Nutrition	(needs serious work)	1 2 3 4 5 6 7 8 9 10	(fully satisfied)
Exercise	(needs serious work)	1 2 3 4 5 6 7 8 9 10	(fully satisfied)
Relationships	(needs serious work)	1 2 3 4 5 6 7 8 9 10	(fully satisfied)
Community	(needs serious work)	1 2 3 4 5 6 7 8 9 10	(fully satisfied)

Overall Finances	(needs serious work)	1 2 3 4 5 6 7 8 9 10	(fully satisfied)
Saving/Investment	(needs serious work)	1 2 3 4 5 6 7 8 9 10	(fully satisfied)
Education	(needs serious work)	1 2 3 4 5 6 7 8 9 10	(fully satisfied)
Creativity	(needs serious work)	1 2 3 4 5 6 7 8 9 10	(fully satisfied)
Stress Management	(needs serious work)	1 2 3 4 5 6 7 8 9 10	(fully satisfied)
Communicating	(needs serious work)	1 2 3 4 5 6 7 8 9 10	(fully satisfied)
Serving Others	(needs serious work)	1 2 3 4 5 6 7 8 9 10	(fully satisfied)
Fun/Adventure	(needs serious work)	1 2 3 4 5 6 7 8 9 10	(fully satisfied)
Recycling Habits	(needs serious work)	1 2 3 4 5 6 7 8 9 10	(fully satisfied)
Other: _____	(needs serious work)	1 2 3 4 5 6 7 8 9 10	(fully satisfied)

EXERCISE

The assessment and following exercise can be seen as your "self-improvement project." This will also help you create your life purpose statement later in the book. In a sense it can be viewed as a self therapy or coaching project as well. You will be gaining new insights on how to change in certain areas of your life by taking concrete actions steps. Exercise: On a new journal page, based on the numbers you circled above, write out each goal and the steps you need to take toward reaching it. Your bolded headings might look something like this: **Domain, Goal, Steps** (with due dates), **Final Due Date.** Carefully consider each one and then go put each of the steps and due date on your calendar. Use a wall size calendar and place it where you have your morning coffee or tea, where you know you will see it every day. By consciously placing the calendar in a convenient place, it will put the goal in your face, lovingly, every day as a good reminder. These practices will help you stay focused and motivated.

STRENGTHS

After you have completed the assessment, note the areas rated in the 8 to 10 range where you are more advanced and feel fully satisfied. These are clear strengths for you. I have not met anyone who does not have at least one area of strength. With the areas rated 5 to 7 you have made good progress but you may wish to evolve yourself to greater satisfaction. Give yourself some time to think about these and what you are willing to go for in terms of personal change. Be realistic with what you can do and prioritize with what is most needed or meaningful to you right now. Also, notice the areas where you need to do some more serious work, 1 to 4, and make some plans to create some positive changes. You might note you don't have far to go in quite a few areas. Or you might recognize you need to get real with your situation, get ready

"If a warrior is to succeed
at anything the success
must come gently, with a
great deal of effort but with
no stress or obsession."
—*Carlos Castaneda*

to roll up your sleeves, get focused, and make some serious changes. I invite you to embrace any and all of these opportunities. Keep your **focus on possibility.** Try envisioning what it will feel like when you have achieved even more success. Ask yourself, "What is it going to take for me to go from a 9 to a 10, or from a 6 to an 8, or from a 1 to a 3?" Make your steps and goals attainable. For example, you are not likely to go from a 1 to a 10 overnight.

I press upon you to recognize that everyone has areas for improvement. Even the most successful coaches and leaders find ways to improve certain areas of their lives. We all need work—we are all a work in progress. As physical beings we are perfectly imperfect, which means that **we get to grow!** Be as open and honest with yourself as you can. You are doing great work!

Add more specific areas to the domains list if you want to take this further. For example, under "self-care" you could add "taking vitamins or herbs" or "meditation practice." You could add "designing a new office space" under creativity, or "writing letters and sending cards" under communicating. Consider the most important areas of life you want to focus on, where you want to learn more, or how you want to be living the life you dream of. The categories, or domains, will become apparent to you as you explore the possibilities of this exercise.

Transcending

"Escher got it right.

Men step down and yet rise up,

the hand is drawn by the hand it draws,

and a woman is poised

on her very own shoulders.

Without you and me this universe is simple,

run with the regularity of a prison.

Galaxies spin along stipulated arcs,

Stars collapse at the specified hour,

Crows u-turn south and monkeys rut on schedule.

But we, whom the cosmos shaped for a billion years

to fit this place, we know it failed.

For we can reshape, reach an arm through the bars,

and, Escher-like, pull ourselves out.

And while whales feeding on mackerel

are confined forever in the sea,

we climb the waves,

look down from clouds."

—From Look Down from Clouds, Marvin Levine, 1997

STRENGTHS AND WEAKNESSES

This section will further help you gain clarity about who you are and where
you are in your life right now, what you love to do, and what you might want
to create. Remember that there is nothing "wrong" with you. We all have
strengths and weaknesses and both of these are gifts
we can learn and grow from. Remember, all of this
is about harnessing your authentic spiritual power
to manifest your true greatness, your true purpose
for being in the physical world.

GOALS

As you have noted above you have some goals to
work on. I want you to consider one of those goals
or something you wish to accomplish. Imagine
a good outcome. What does it look like? What
does it feel like? This next step is very important.
Consider the obstacles that might get in your way.
Then ensure that you devise a plan for overcoming
the obstacles.

EXERCISE

On a separate journal page, list your
strengths and weaknesses. You can make
this as long as you want. Listing your
strengths and weaknesses is another way
to consider how you perceive yourself and
what to work on. Your headers can be
bolded such as: **Strengths** (Fabulous Me!)
and **Weaknesses** (Golden opportunities
for change).

"Change will not come
if we wait for some other
person or some other time.
We are the ones we've been
waiting for. We are the
change that we seek."
—*President Barak Obama*

Along with the positive mental imaging you must also consider any potential drawbacks, hooks, snares, or quicksand in the way of getting what you want. Having an optimistic mindset about the future is not unrealistic dreaming and it is more than imagination. But to dream and forecast failure is important to motivation and setting realistic goals.

Remember this formula: dream+plan+act+learn+re-work-the-plan+determination=successful goal attainment.

EXERCISE

Ask yourself if you are ready to cross the bridge into the next stage of your life. Can you commit to the road ahead? I invite you to picture yourself walking across that bridge in your mind's eye—confident, prepared, and focused for what lies ahead.

CHAPTER 8: TO CLEAN

To live a spiritually-based or heart-centered life and to move forward in life you have to get out of your own way. You do this by cleaning up things from the past, which will be the focus of the next few chapters. If you do not clean and tidy things up regularly, you remain stagnant or stuck, like a sailboat with no wind. You might find yourself bouncing back and forth in the waves of life repeating the same old patterns. The consequence is that you may not allow the momentum of life to move you forward; you could end up on someone else's course or adrift on chaotic seas unfocused and living a life you never intended. I say earnestly to you that you must command the helm of the ship of you—no one else is going to do this for you. Remain vigilantly yet warmly aware of your calling and work through all of the lessons so you can **get your genius ON!**

Once you have cleaned up the past, you can start to **groove with life in a more organic way.** Your energy will be contagious—it's the kind of meaningful connection people want to experience more of in the world. But each person has to do their own healing work to make it happen. I know you really want to glide with the waves of your life. How might you boogie, jive, jam, and sway more with all of life?

Here's the thing, **you can't keep playing small or smallish.** In addition to claiming your spiritual truth and living from that place, you have to **decide if you are going to make your life happen by activating your God-given talents and skills.** Cleaning up will allow you

EXERCISE

Ask yourself, "How do I want my life to look and feel different from the way it does now?" Take some time to journal your thoughts before proceeding.

"Gardening is a metaphor for life, teaching you to nourish new life and weed out that which cannot succeed."
—*Nelson Mandela*

to move in that direction. Your growth toward success will be determined by your level of **motivation, dedication, and desire in all phases**. Check in with yourself right now about your willingness to go deeper.

TENDING THE GARDEN

Now I invite you to weed and prune the garden of your past, and to dig a bit. To uncover and compost the old energy will require some TLC. You are being asked to not only peek into the past, but dig down to clear out where you have been collecting waste and toxins (literal stress in your body) and turn it into healthy, productive energy.

You are encouraged to do this carefully and mindfully. You must look at the pain, the old stories, hurts, disappointments, the negative patterns, and unhealthy habits—look all experience square in the eye, embrace it, love it for all it came here to teach you, and then boldly release it so new buds can spring forth. Just as those tropical rainstorms in Hawaii always bring forth new gorgeous blossoms, you can bloom and create abundance in all areas of your life.

I love to gaze into Hawaiian flowers, especially the soft plumeria, proud protea, the elegant ginger, and the brilliant bird of paradise. And I love the scent of gardenia. What flower do you love? Can you imagine your life unfurling into the world as your favorite flower?

You are capable of totally renewing yourself. Hold this absolute knowing in your heart. Know this too—living your greatest life depends on cleaning up, clearing, and maintaining the fruitful gardens of you. Let's take this a step further.

HANU (BREATHING)

All of the cleaning begins with practicing your hanu (breathing). This may sound odd at first, but the process of conscious breathing is where so much of cleaning up the past and attaining your life goals begins. Your life began when your mother gave birth to you, and the very first thing you did was to breathe into life effortlessly. What a gift! You will be able to clean up your mind and all of the past, and be able to manage all of the challenges in life so much better when you become aware of your breathing.

Becoming aware of your breathing helps you to concentrate and create transformation in your life. To help make this point I turn again to author and Vietnamese Buddhist Monk, Thich Nhat Hanh. He shows us this type of mindful breathing creates the liberating power of insight. He says, "Concentration helps us focus on just one thing. With concentration, the energy of looking becomes more powerful, and insight is possible. Insight always has the power of liberating us. If mindfulness is there, and we know how to keep mindfulness alive, concentration will be there, too. And if we know how to keep concentration alive, insight will come also. The energy of mindfulness enables us to look deeply and gain the insight we need so that transformation is possible." He also says, "Breath is the bridge that connects life to consciousness, the bridge that unites your body to your thoughts. Whenever your mind becomes scattered, use your breath as the means to take hold of your mind again."

You have been practicing becoming aware of your thoughts, and now you will incorporate that practice as you begin to notice your breathing. The good thing about this is that it is natural. Do you know that there is a larger Source that actually breathes you? Author Eckhart Tolle tells us, "The coming into manifestation of the world as well as its return to the unmanifested—its expansion and contraction—are two universal movements that we could call the out-going and the return home. Those two movements are reflected throughout the universe in many ways, such as in the incessant expansion and contraction of your heart, as well as in the inhalation and exhalation of your breath." What a lovely spiritual gift. Your very act of breathing is like the back and forth of the waves. It is essentially effortless, and it is free. The practice of meditation slows you down so you can consciously breathe and get into the rise and fall, the cadence, of your Source.

ʻŌKUPU

ʻŌkupu is an ancient Hawaiian style of meditation. According to the website okupu.com, "ʻŌkupu is deeply rooted in the traditional wisdom and aloha of nā kūpuna—the elders and ancestors of Hawaiʻi. ʻŌkupu means 'To sprout, as seeds; to come forth, as clouds.'" As described further on the site,

*"Aloha is primordial, unconditional love. 'Ōkupu meditation
reveals this clearly, offering a direct perception of aloha
expressing itself as the universal creative force, the vibrant
wellspring of existence. As we direct our attention inward, we
are immersed in Spirit and connected to our infinite source.
This experience becomes the natural focus of meditation."*

In the practice of 'Ōkupu, practitioners may also incorporate traditional healing arts such as Huaka'i Akakū (spirit journeying) and 'Ōlelo A'o Loko (talks
and discussions) to help prepare for and support the experience of meditation.

Try this guided imagery: Close your eyes. Simply breathe. Just note your
in-breath and out-breath. Imagine your favorite flower again as mentioned
above. Maybe it is a proud pink protea, a white peace lilly, a happy yellow
daisy, a bright orange poppy, a deep purple violet,
or a crimson red hibiscus. Whatever you choose,
with eyes closed, bring that flower closer in your
mind's eye. Name your flower out loud. Stay with
the experience. Now acknowledge that you are in
the process of unfolding much like your favorite
flower, and that with each breath, you open a little
more. You are contracting and expanding, and you
are feeling what that feels like, deep in your body,
as your organs, bones, blood, and all of your cells
are working together to expand who you are. Note

EXERCISE

Stop for a moment and read the following
guided imagery once, then go back and
allow yourself to experience the guided
imagery itself. You could also record it
and script it to fit your preferences, or take
turns reading it with a trusted friend.

the colors, fragrance, textures, and the complete essence of this flower. Be
at one with this flower. Breathe. You have become one with this flower. You
have firm roots, and you are grounded. At the same time you are opening
and reaching, effortlessly, and your breathing allows you to immerse yourself
in the experience of oneness. You are living, being, growing, expanding, and
simply allowing the process to unfold naturally, as you surrender. Try to let
any unrelated thoughts pass through as if on a ticker tape and return to your
connection with the flower.

You are held by the Earth. The sunshine and the rain nourish you. Continue to breathe naturally. Your breathing is continually renewing you, and your body is dancing with delight that you are consciously creating the life you were meant to be living, right here and now. Take three more breaths then gently open your eyes and return to normal consciousness.

Whether or not you call your conscious breathing a practice in meditation, when you stop to breathe deeply, you purposely slow down and become more mindful of life. In this act, you are allowing more oxygen to flow into your cells. Breathing is an act of cleansing.

THE MIRACLE OF BREATH

I have used guided imagery and simple meditation breathing techniques with my coaching clients and with my patients in the clinical and medical setting. They use it to help with stress and anxiety, to prepare for surgery, and to cope with loss. It helps them to relax and to consciously send blood to certain parts of the body to assist with healing physical ailments.

Stopping to consciously breathe helps you move through challenging situations and stretch beyond your troubles or strife. Conscious breathing connects you to your soul, to God, Buddha, intuition, nature, spirit. Whatever name you choose for this energy is fine. It is the **deep connection** that matters.

Every single act of breathing is a miracle—and miracles come in many forms. A miracle can be a divine idea, making a choice from your soul versus your ego, or a huge shift in the way you see something. The conversion of a negative thought to a positive thought is a miracle. Miracles are everywhere, and if you are aware enough to note them, you can live in a space of synchronicity and miracles. Slow down enough to notice the miracles. You, too, are a miracle! Like the flower experience you tried above, allow your breathing to "take you there" and note the miracles in you and all around you as you walk through your days.

BREATH, THOUGHTS, AND EMOTIONS AS ENERGY

In a graduation speech that appears on dailygood.org, Nipun Mehta tells us,

"Your state of being inherently affects my state of being. And
we do have science to prove this. Research has shown that in
close proximity, when people feel connected, their individual
heartbeats start to synchronize, even with no physical contact.
In neuroscience, the discovery of 'mirror neurons' has shown
us that we literally do feel each other's pains, and joys."

Consider a shared smile. A smile from one person usually elicits a smile in another. Over the next few days try to practice smiling more as you pass by people on the sidewalk or in a hallway and see what type of response you get.

Pause to note your breathing in this moment. Breathing is energy. When you are consciously in touch with breathing energy, feeling the waves of goodness and greatness—and the deep abiding love that comes from it—then you are seriously affecting those around you too. The more tuned in you are, even as you move through the regular routines of your days, you serve those around you by being the higher vibration the world needs. Can you see how powerful the act of conscious breathing is?

The act of unconscious breathing is powerful too, but for different reasons. When one is consciously breathing and practicing from a place of authenticity, the energy levels are higher. That is a **love vibration.** When one is not consciously breathing, the energy levels are lower, perhaps even in a depressed state. Haven't you walked into a room and "felt the energy"? I think we all have. Just as the physical world requires energy, everything happening inside of us requires energy as well.

Thoughts and emotions are energetic. You think of something you want to accomplish, something of great importance to you. But instead of seeing a clear way to accomplish your goal, and being instilled with the confidence that such clarity brings,

EXERCISE

First, say "mahalo, hanu" (thank you, breath). Now, in this moment, stop and notice how you are breathing. Try to breathe in through your nose and out through your mouth. Feel your belly rise, then your chest rise on the in-breath. Then slightly open your mouth on the exhale. Next, note your thoughts as you breathe. Try to stay focused on the in-breath and the out-breath. Random thoughts will come up but try to let them go. Just say to yourself, "breathing," "hanu," or "aloha." Then return to the in-breath—belly expands, chest expands—and exhale through the mouth.

your mind automatically focuses on the negatives and the possibility of failure. Next thing you know, fear has made the goal seem impossible to attain. But you can learn to counter such negative thoughts with positive thoughts—the force of which overcomes your fears.

This is the same for emotions as well. You can change your thoughts and you can change your emotions. The idea here is that through your choices you can have more authentically powerful, good, kind, purposeful energy benefiting yourself and the greater good of all. Or you could have lower level energy emanating from a worried, depressed, burned out, valueless, meaningless, fearful, hateful, or egoic state. Which do you prefer? It is likely we all would choose higher energy states once we consciously realize we have these options. Can we all get better at practicing this? You bet!

Now let's get you practicing your mindful breathing some more so you can increase the good feeling-energy vibrations and clean out the old energies.

I will go more in depth with meditation techniques later on. For now, try consciously breathing many times per day no matter where you are or what you are doing.

STOPPING TO GO

I have read that in Buddhist practice we must stop to breathe, slowing down as we sit in meditation, so we can speed up when we need to, and get on with the meaningful things in our lives. When we allow for this time, we have the energy to do more of the things that truly matter to us, and we make better choices. We become more focused and productive, and live with greater meaning.

Consider areas in your life where you think you could slow down and become more mindful, so you can open up to greater focus and intention in other areas. I highly recommend *The Mind's Own Physician*, by Jon Kabat-Zinn, Ph.D., and Richard J. Davidson, Ph.D., which gives the scientific evidence for the effectiveness of meditation. It also contains a dialogue with the Dalai Lama on the healing power of meditation and cites numerous professional articles.

Give thanks for the breath of life every morning. Honor and remember your **conscious breathing** as much as you can every day. This is a wonderful act of cleaning your body and mind, the temple, the house, the marvelous mansion, and the vibrant, lush gardens of you!

CLEANING PHYSICAL SPACE

I also invite you to consider the physical space in your life. Cleaning this space can also help you clear up your mind. Think about each room in your home and what you need to let go of. Clear out the clutter to clear your mind, and the energy space all around you. See if you can keep out only a few inspiring objects to remind you of your goals, your dreams, and your new view of life.

EXERCISE

Choose one area in your living space this week that really needs your attention and commit to it. Block a few hours of time on your calendar right now. Then write a to-do list including what you plan to clear, clean, re-organize, or de-clutter. Consider re-arranging furniture if you are inspired to.

"A quiet mind is all you need. All else will happen rightly, once your mind is quiet. As the sun on rising makes the world active, so does self-awareness affect change, in the mind. In the light of calm and steady self-awareness inner energies wake up and work miracles without effort on your part."
—*Sri Nisargatta Maharaj*

CHAPTER 9: FORGIVENESS

If you have worked through the previous chapters, you are now prepared for one of the most profound ways of moving beyond your old self, your pain, and your old stories. We all experience times in life when we feel hurt or betrayed by someone. These feelings are a part of being human. But the liberating truth is that we have a choice about what we do with our feelings. In this chapter you are going to look at the dark stuff to give yourself a deep cleaning. This opens you up to the light wanting to come forth. **Forgiveness is *the* healing process that creates freedom for living and loving deeply.** Rather than hold on to resentment or anger, you can actively choose to forgive. Forgiveness can even change you on a cellular level by releasing the stress that has built up from harboring resentments, pain, and grievances. The act of forgiveness frees up space within and allows more room for healing, appreciation, love, and happiness. This is a meaty chapter, so go ahead and roll up your sleeves.

Remember the analogy of the acrobat bar that you were invited to use earlier in the book? I encouraged you to kalele (trust) in the process that was being laid out for you, to begin releasing that imagined acrobat bar so you could open up to newer levels of your being (to the new bar on its way to you). I am asking you to open up once again.

In the previous chapter you were introduced to conscious breathing as a mechanism for cleaning up. It is helpful to use your breathing as you consider the challenges of this chapter as well.

It is also important to think about forgiving those who may have wronged you and letting go of the negative experiences you cling to. They hold you under the water, attempting to drown you, preventing you from riding the waves of your life with greater joy and resiliency. You have to be willing to get honest about all of the un-forgiveness that you might be holding.

Dr. Jampolsky, author of *Forgiveness Is the Greatest Healer of All,* taught me that before we can immerse ourselves in the practice of forgiving, it is important to know what forgiveness is not…

- Forgiveness is not about justifying anyone's hurtful or painful behaviors of any kind.

- Forgiveness is not about forgetting or sweeping anything under the rug.

- Forgiveness is not the same as reconciliation.

- Forgiveness is not about the other person.

I was a volunteer and eventually became the Director at Dr. Jampolsky's International Center for Attitudinal Healing in Sausalito, CA. The name of the organization changed, but Dr. Jampolsky's legacy Attitudinal Healing programs were still active. One time, Dr. Jampolsky told me, "Melissa, you have to let go of your anger at that person. He was only doing the best he could in that moment, given his state of consciousness at that time. You have got to free yourself." I had been walking around harboring so much anger toward an individual for what I perceived to be a community tragedy. I experienced painful headaches and began to eat too much ice cream to escape from the hurt that I was feeling. I was making myself sick with my negative attitude, trying to eat my way through the upset and staying stuck in my un-forgiveness story. It was Dr. Jampolsky's comment that helped me know what I needed to do to get back on track. So I did. I went in deep with forgiving and feeling my feelings. The truth is that it took me several years to fully move through my pain on that issue. You can do this work as well. Don't worry about the time frame. Just know that each person is on her own path. The important thing is to get started. Below are a few powerful definitions of forgiveness.

FORGIVENESS IS...

- Forgiveness is letting go of resentment and anger.

- Forgiveness is a choice.

- Forgiveness is about giving up all hopes for a better past.

- Forgiveness is your ticket to heal yourself.

- Forgiveness is a process.

- Forgiveness is an "inside" job.

- Forgiveness is necessary when you decide that you want to heal and no longer suffer.

In all of my readings and teaching workshops on forgiveness, I now see clearly that forgiveness frees us and propels us into living a fully interconnected life. It reminds me that we are responsible for freeing ourselves and that we all affect the whole of life all of the time, whether we choose to forgive or not.

PAINS BECOME GIFTS

When I arrived in Hawaii at age eleven, I didn't know that something was just starting to become activated in me, something important. It was as if the story of my past life in the South was being swept out to sea and I was getting "cleared" for the adventure ahead. There were moments when I wished the air had taken that extra large baggage of suffering and sent it hurling into the vast Pacific Ocean.

Instead, I got to work through every last bit of it...every dirty, rotten, ugly piece of the painful past including the early loss of my father, my early death bed experience, the poverty, malnutrition, family alcoholism and depression, and the multiple moves. It would take a long time, after listening to many other stories of forgiveness, and setting my own forgiveness work into motion, that I would come to know these pains as a huge gift that contributed toward my growth and my overall happiness.

"Beyond our anger lies our capacity to forgive. Forgiveness is looking at people with the spiritual knowledge of their innocence rather than the mortal perception of their guilt. Forgiveness is a radical act, but

it is certainly not weakness.
By forgiving, we do not grant
victory to those who wronged
us: instead we surrender
the aspect of mind that is
blocking divine correction."
—*Marianne Williamson*

EXERCISE

Stop for a moment. If it feels comfortable to you, affirm for yourself, "I absolutely know I have what it takes to work on forgiving. I am worthy of freedom. I am willing to set this process in motion."

I hope you are able to embrace the forgiveness teachings and exercises outlined for you below and work through your pains and wounds. Call forth **fearlessness** to clear yourself and cleanse your whole being to lift yourself into higher dimensions.

As a teacher of forgiveness, I came to see the importance of sharing forgiveness stories, both for my own healing and as a witness to many clients and patients. The shared stories especially help when you are first getting started.

RELEASE VICTIMHOOD

At one time I was a volunteer consultant with the World Wide Forgiveness Alliance in Corte Madera, California. The organization was started by a wonderful man, a friend of mine, attorney Bob Plath. Bob and I led forgiveness groups in a residential treatment facility in Marin County. I witnessed women choosing to forgive perpetrators for hateful crimes, and to forgive themselves for atrocious acts as well. I observed vulnerable people, angry people, confused and depressed people, addicts, mothers, sisters, and daughters all heal from catastrophic situations. At the end of a group guided imagery exercise, one woman said she saw herself as a monster. Later, when I had asked them to picture themselves in a mirror, the same woman said she could only see herself as a child, because that is when she last remembered being innocent. She was that child deep down inside, and she was able to tap into that innocence again, and to hold and nurture it. The experience allowed her to step into the mature and wise woman she is today.

EXERCISE

Take a few deep breaths. Reflect and answer the following questions in your journal.

1. In what areas of my life do I need to practice forgiveness?

2. What might I be holding on to from the past that keeps me stuck?

3. What do I get if I choose not to forgive?

This woman particularly benefited from the group as she began to shed tears, moving beyond her past and her shame, and being vulnerable enough

"Forgiveness is the fragrance that the violet sheds on the heel that has crushed it."
—*Mark Twain*

"We cannot change the past, but we can change our attitude toward it. Uproot guilt and plant forgiveness. Tear out arrogance and seed humility. Exchange love for hate, thereby, making the present more comfortable and the future promising."
—*Maya Angelou*

to demonstrate courage and healing to others. She began to forgive herself and her perpetrator. She began to release her victimhood and open to her true power. She represents what we are all capable of and need to do, no matter the level of pain that we might be experiencing.

The following exercises are a part of the forgiveness process I teach in my workshop intensives and now you can try them.

THE STORY

Think of anything you still might hold an attitude of unforgiveness toward. It is important you allow yourself some "get real" time as you consider the power of forgiveness. These situations could have happened five minutes ago, or twenty five years ago. Be honest with yourself, even if this is painful and difficult. Remember, you are doing this to **free yourself**.

Drawing again from Marianne Williamson:

> *"We forgive, then, out of self-interest. I forgive you because*
> *I want out of my pain. I forgive you so that I can be free*
> *of what you did. I see beyond your mistake to the love*
> *in you so that I can see beyond the mistake to the love in*
> *me—because only then can I have a miracle. The universe*
> *will immediately reprogram itself to send us miracles,*
> *when we remove the barriers to our willingness to love.*
> *Forgiveness is the most powerful key to new beginnings."*

No one wants to remain in a state of pain and suffering. We all want to be free. Remember **you are not your past**. You are not any "story" that keeps you tied to thinking or behaving a certain way whether it happened recently or in the past. There are many things we have all been through, and we have all suffered many types of losses, so **you are not alone**. We have all suffered, and we have all had innumerable stressful experiences. Some of us have had more than our share! Remember, whatever it was, or whatever it is, you are not those things or situations. You are not the divorce. You are not the death. You are not the old job. You are not the poverty. You are not the physical illness. You are not the mental illness. You are not the "black sheep."

"Even after all this time, the
sun never says to the Earth,
'You owe me.' Look what
happens with a love like that.
It lights the whole sky."
—Hafiz

"Behold not with anger the sins of man, but forgive and cleanse."
—*Queen Lili'uokalani*

You are not the physical pain. You are not the money. You are not the house. You are not the child. You are not the broken home. You are not the breakup. You are not the diagnosis. You are not the prognosis. Complete this sentence for yourself, "I am not the (blank), (blank), or (blank)." Fill in the blanks with the main issue(s) you have been holding onto and wish to release.

You are a miracle. You are capable of receiving miracles and creating miracles. Your choices can be miraculous. By choosing to forgive, you create a miracle for yourself. Affirm this sentence for yourself by stating it out loud, **"I am a miracle. I am worthy of miracles. I can choose the miracle."**

By forgiving whatever and whomever, you are releasing old energy and opening yourself up to new beginnings, new ways of choosing for yourself, and of navigating the world. Forgiving allows you to die to old ways of thinking, seeing, and being in the world. You allow healing to take place so you can move forward with life. You are releasing the acrobat bar and opening up to the new goodness that is already on its way to you, now.

OPEN TO LOVE

Dr. Jampolsky also taught me that at any given time we are all either operating from fear or from love. Forgiveness gets us to face our fears and moves us into love. By choosing forgiveness we choose to get out of the wake of our past, the wake of the ego self, and the wake of the ideas others have for us so that we can be open to love in all of its forms. From love the heart creates vibrations and harmonies. Those electrical nerve impulses are processed by your senses so you can make more loving impressions on your whole being when you choose love. From this space we all can lovingly, confidently, and joyfully row our own boats far out from the harbors of fear. We choose every moment of every day from this space, either coming from love or fear. I'd much rather that my life be a manifestion of love! What would you rather be?

I recommend Dr. Jampolsky's *New York Times* best selling classic book, *Love Is Letting Go of Fear*. In it he writes, "When we cherish grievances we allow our mind to be fed by fear and we become imprisoned by these distortions." He goes on to say, "We need to remind ourselves constantly that Love is the only reality there is." Perhaps you will grab the helm and choose to fully experience the forgiveness process so you can float across the powerful waters of your life, in charge, co-creating, and being the dynamic life force of healing power that the world needs. Can you see how the world needs you to forgive, deeply, passionately—releasing, cleaning up, once and for all, so you can claim and live your greatness? Can you see how **the whole world needs your love,** too?

THE STORY OF EVA KOR

Even larger social, political, and historical events can require forgiveness. In my coaching classes, I often share a story chronicled in a documentary film, *Forgiving Dr. Mangele,* which followed a courageous woman named Eva Kor back to Germany after the end of World War II. She knew in her heart that she had to forgive the Nazi doctors who experimented on her and her twin sister during the Holocaust. Eva's sister died at the hands of the doctors. Eva knew this was a sensitive topic for many. Yet she also knew the pain and suffering she clung to was killing her life energy. She wanted to free her mind so she could step into living the life that she had been given. Eva found one Nazi doctor who admitted to war crimes, and she was able to meet him face to face to state her forgiveness toward him. This gave her power to heal from her loss and her painful story. This does not mean Eva was trying to forget her sister or what they endured. But it did mean she was trying to heal so she could live with more peace in her life. Eva went on to help mediate international peace talks, and she opened her own Holocaust Remembrance Center. Eva's story of forgiveness is a perfect example of how you can release yourself from un-forgiveness and from extreme violation or horrific pain. She learned to **face and embrace** the pain. She then released it and used the lessons in powerful ways to help others.

Just as Eva did, I encourage you to **keep letting go of fear and step further into love.** Allow the issues of life to pass through you. Send

EXERCISE

Answer the following questions in your journal.

1. What are the gifts that I receive when I forgive?
2. Who can I forgive, and for what?
3. What situation(s) do I need to release?
4. What small things in my life need forgiving?
5. What are the larger issues that I need to forgive?

them love as you envision toxic energies on their way out. You have evolved way beyond survival instincts. Can you commit to freeing yourself from the scared person inside?

HO'OPONOPONO

In Hawaii some people continue to practice Ho'oponopono. It means, "to edit." It is also an ancient Hawaiian problem-solving process that involves just one thing: forgiving. The word Ho'oponopono has several additional meanings such as "to set right" and "mental cleansing." In ancient times, the family elder would call the family to a conference so they could resolve whatever conflict the parties were having—sibling rivalry, for example. The goal would be to have everyone involved be heard.

This process might include prayer, discussion, confession, repentance, and mutual restitution. No one was allowed to get up from the family circle until forgiveness had been expressed. At the completion of the ceremony, they might share a Hala flower lei, and then they would share a meal. How might you adopt a similar ritual for forgiveness in your own family, or among friends?

FROM STORY TO GLORY

I once clung to the very sad and depressing story that my father died when I was only four and a half, and that he left my mom and me to struggle through life. Part of that "story" included me being on my deathbed at an early age and being raised in a very poor, uneducated part of the South.

At that time, still seeing myself as a victim, I could not grasp an authentic notion of God. After doing my forgiveness work, however, I came to know my father's early death as both a huge loss and one of the greatest gifts of my life. I started to focus on the gift. My own early deathbed illness also gifted me by helping me to be resilient and to appreciate every single day. I had to do my work though! Forgiveness helped me open up and understand that God didn't give me anything I could not handle. I believe God wanted me to go through all of it so I could be strong and compassionate for others going through enormous change and loss. This is, in part, why I started a life coaching practice, and it is one reason why I continue to work as a medical professional helping people manage their physical changes, face end of life issues, and embrace living their legacies.

By moving from your old stories, you can **let your sails soar, open your heart, and embrace your glory!**

Have you thought about the stories you need to address? Whether they are stories you constantly repeat in the presence of others, or those in your own mind, it is time to go head to head with each one. Remember that these could involve a constant tale of "woe is me," "why me," "they did," "he said," or even trauma or abuse from the past. Be bold with this and **switch your bravery button on**.

Now you are being invited to write your un-forgiveness stories. Write out everything that comes up in terms of your pain and suffering, the wounds, scars, the hurt, and the losses. Be real and raw with yourself. And be sure to let the feelings surface as you write. Swear in your writing if you need to. Cry buckets if you need to. Just don't drown in the bucket. If you feel overwhelmed with your feelings, you might want to consider professional psychotherapy. Many people need help getting out of the bucket, so be honest with yourself. One way to gauge if you are drowning in the bucket is if you are not able to get out of bed in the mornings, if you feel helpless or hopeless, or if you are crying uncontrollably and it interferes with your daily life.

> # EXERCISE
>
>
>
> Get out your journal. Consider an issue or person you need to forgive. Write out the unforgiveness story first. Write about your anger, pain, fears, your reaction, and your suffering. Do this for each issue of un-forgiveness that you still cling to.

RE-SCRIPT

Remember, **the process of forgiveness can be the most freeing thing you ever have done for yourself,** even if it feels challenging. Take as much time as you need to with this exercise. When you are finished writing, you may need to take a relaxing bath, or go for a walk. Do something that feels good to your soul. I can tell you from having re-scripted many stories that the only way through the pain is to feel into it—allow your feelings to

EXERCISE

Here is the "fun" part of doing your forgiveness work. You get to re-write and re-script the story into a new one. You get to find the gifts in your pains, and you get to re-name it and claim it. So, go back and re-write your un-forgiveness stories into new stories. The new story is about identifying the learning, the insights, the inspiration, the understandings, or the new identity that may have come as a result of the experiences.

emerge, note them, and name them. Learn to **lean into** this process—that's the only way you can begin to release that which no longer serves you. You might feel lighter as you embrace the darkness, the pain, the suffering…even as you are deeply immersed in it. You become more consciously aware of working through things. The more you practice forgiveness (since more challenges will surely come), you might be able to move through them more quickly. Life will still bring rough times, but if you remain on course doing your inner work, you can continue to forgive and find greater happiness.

"The first medicine is forgiveness. Before any one of us can heal ourselves we need to have forgiveness. We need to have pono (balance). If we cannot forgive ourselves, we cannot heal others, we cannot heal anyone."

—*Kapuna Alapa'I Kahu'ena, La'au Lapa'au (Herbal Practitioner, Oahu)*

Act II. Diving In

CHAPTER 10: ALOHA EGO

In Act I you completed the prescriptive awakening, clarifying, and clearing work. In Act II it is time to move into accepting the changes that are taking place deep within your psyche and your soul. This requires that you have made sufficient efforts in previous chapters. However, if you happen to have any remaining forgiveness work to do, this chapter will offer you another opportunity.

At this point, if you are doing the work I have laid out for you, you are probably noticing how great you feel on many levels. You are probably making some necessary shifts in your whole being. Your energy is shifting—you feel it on a cellular level, yet people around you may get a different impression of you and respond to you differently. You will need to deal with those who view your changed personality to be negative. This may create some trepidation or this is where all hell can break loose because even though you can be feeling great, it is easy to get caught up in fears, your own, and others'…and all of it is about the ego.

ALOHA EGO (INTRODUCTION TO THE PROCESS)

I have designed a way to help you manage all of this. This is a strategy that I call "Aloha Ego," which you will learn how to use later in this chapter. We will look at games of the ego, the importance of rowing your own boat, and drawing healthy boundaries. Then we will go into defining the ego and how to tame it. This stage of accepting puts you at a critical juncture where you must decide whether or not you will dive in to continue to do the "real hard work," so to speak, and engage further with this process. Any ambivalence you might be experiencing is normal. If you do not feel ready to dive in from the top, are you at least ready to find a better starting point, then scoot yourself to the edge and slowly lower yourself down until you feel a bit more comfortable? It might help to practice that **trusting muscle** that I have been reminding you about. Envision the new trapeze bar coming your way, and that you are confidently releasing the old bar as you trust and focus on grabbing the new one. **Remain willing**, then allow your higher power, your Source (as you have been defining it) to guide you.

EGO GAMES

The tragedy of 9-11 proved to be a serious turning point in my life. Earlier I mentioned that a very dear friend of mine perished on flight 93 that went down near Pittsburgh. I was living in San Francisco and was pretty far off from my spiritual course. I was in between jobs—thinking of leaving my career, trying to follow the crowd, and lost in materialism. For several years I would try new jobs and take temporary jobs outside of doing professional social work because I thought I needed to be like others who appeared to have it all. They were friends or friends of friends mainly working in business or sales. They travelled frequently, drove nice cars and enjoyed the good life. That was in fact pretty good for them from where I sat. But for me, what a game! Those attempts at career change always proved unfulfilling because I was doing it for the wrong reasons. My ego was working over time. In hindsight, I learned a lot in the course of shifting out of my "what's in it for me?" and "money defines my worth" attitudes because they were never ever a true part of me.

How might you have played similar games? How might you find yourself currently running with the herd?

The events of 9-11 made me stop and think about my life, my true purpose in the world, and the interconnectedness of all things. The tragedy of that day

> # EXERCISE
>
>
>
> Imagine yourself taking a walk along a white sandy beach and consider if you are headed confidently in the direction YOU TRULY DESIRE...

got me on a path of accepting that I needed to focus on the right things and to stop letting my ego trip me up.

ROW YOUR OWN BOAT

I am glad I tried new things with work because I learned a lot, especially about what I truly value and about my real worth. Once I got on a spiritual path, I found work with organizations that resonated with my values. I would slowly but surely get to the next higher paying position, and eventually the next.

Years later I realized that if I had been tapped into how my ego was at work earlier on, I would not have wasted so much time. Back then, however, I wasn't connected to enough heart centered people. I wasn't hanging out with my real tribe. I don't beat myself up about that now. That is just what needed to occur so I could learn and grow. The point is, though, that once you understand what your ego is and how to manage it, your life will take a very different course also.

The ego is a fascinating human construct. Initially I needed to learn to get in touch with my ego, to be aware of it, and befriend it, so I could begin to operate primarily from my heart with gratitude and appreciation. Once I began to do that, life just started to show up to me and then I was rowing my own boat and connecting to my real crew. That meant that I was staying more in tune with my inner desires and less with the desires of those around me. I started to embody my truth for being and living a liberated life.

Have you had times when you shifted out of living from your ego mode? How did life change for you? Do you want to row your own boat, and what does that mean to you now?

SHIFTING

The lessons on ego management tend to be challenging because things are shifting around you. You are shifting spiritually and therefore those very close to you may be noting that you're different, somehow. You probably care very much for these people, and they might even be some of your own family members. When you begin to take your personal transformation seriously, oftentimes this means that you end up moving away from those people who do not genuinely support your growth. You might be inclined to move closer into the circles of people who truly care and empower your evolution. Others might try to make you think that your changes are bad or strange or go against tradition. They are likely just projecting their own feelings of insecurity and worthlessness onto you. They might be trying to guilt trip you. And it is because they don't understand; they are scared and confused about who they really are in the world. Their egos are acting out, but you are not responsible for the way they think and feel, and you are certainly not responsible for their egos. Try not to let yourself be concerned with their opinions about you. It might also be best to keep your progress to yourself with most people. **This is an opportunity for you to practice compassion and send them silent blessings**, to claim your own space to continue on this path—**your path of greatness.** It might feel like you are alone on your path at times, which is normal. You do, in fact, sometimes forget where you come from and who walks beside you, that Source by whatever name you have given it. **Keep returning to your truth** amidst the lunacy that people might try to throw your way and try to connect more with your real clan.

I like to remind myself of the following affirmation: "I am not the storms (ego), and I am not the darkness (ego). This person or situation has only come to teach me, and to put me back on course." While it is life that requires us to get off course so we learn, the goal of living a spiritually centered life is really to **get back on course** sooner rather than later and to put those lessons to good use.

BOUNDARIES

In this section, I offer you ways to help you weather your ego's harsh winds, the wild storms and the hurricanes of life, including those that others try to put in your path.

As I've mentioned, I do not want you to get stuck in the ego junk of others, or wallow in thoughts like, "How is my transformation going to make them feel if I become more spiritual or even more successful in my life?" One strategy can be to claim your own sacred space by distancing from certain people in order to thrive. I am not saying that you have to be hurtful or mean to others as you claim your space and make changes, but you probably will have to face the challenge of disconnecting from those who are not supporting you in healthy ways. Creating healthy boundaries in this way can help you heal and achieve your goals. This is also how you shine as an example to others.

There are a few options for creating your boundaries with negative or toxic people. You can invite some people to have open, loving conversations about your respective needs and then, in a sincere and open conversation, lovingly release them as you each go separate ways. Or you can silently walk away from people who would not understand, or who would create drama and stress. Who knows, this might be a gift to them as well. The point is that you can't be responsible for their feelings or how they might react.

> ## EXERCISE
>
>
>
> Affirm out loud: "I can absolutely weather the storms of my life."

In this chapter, as promised, you will also explore how you might need to tie up any loose ends with the forgiveness work. By doing this, you can determine limits you set with others.

NO STOPPING POINT

By saying "aloha" to your ego, you are accepting your innate ability to make **lasting significant changes** in your life—which will affect everyone around you. Those who are open will be affected positively, and those who remain closed will stay their course until they are ready to make a shift. It is good to know this; since your inner work is never really "done," you get to play with and tame your ego over and over again, so it's best to start taming it now. This is how you evolve.

Knowing that one's inner work is never really complete is the core of the acceptance I want to convey in this chapter. By taming the ego, you find that you can move through the tough times more quickly and move away from those who do not understand you or who would not back you up. There is no stopping point, and there is no "finish line" to get to. **Spiritual work, or life mastery work, is a process, and you can start to integrate the attitude that by being bold and by feeling the fear, you can move forward in spite of it.**

I created the "Aloha Ego" practice as a fun way to manage my daily stressors and to increase my mindfulness and heart-centeredness. As I've mentioned above, the word "aloha" has many meanings in the Hawaiian language. These include, "hello," "love," and "good-bye." These are the three meanings that work for the practice I have designed. I have been using these in my life coaching workshops and classes for years. People tell me they love it, and they really do seem to be enjoying it as I observe them immersed in the work.

DEFINING EGO

Before you go into the Aloha Ego process, make sure you are clear on what the ego is. Ego is the part of the personality that is separate, resisting, competitive, vain, whiney, self-centered, fearful, self-absorbed, material, and loves a good pity party. Ego is the annoying internal chatter that says, "I want to be right, and better, than others, and I will be so at any cost." Ego thrives on drama. Ego is sarcastic and puts others down. Ego does not want you to forgive. Ego does not want you to be mindful, loving, kind, or generous. Ego is the negative self-talk that says, "I am not good enough, thin enough, or smart enough." Ego loves to blame others or make them look bad. Ego often wants more material things, more food, more booze, more sex, more money, more fame, more of anything, and all for the wrong reasons. Ego is very fear based, withholding, and controlling. Ego unfortunately permeates our society. Ego causes wars (both internal and external), conflict, and violence. Ego is the "cut off" part of the true self. Ego views the world through the eyes of limitation. Ego tells you what you cannot do, and says you are bad, wrong, and unworthy—but Ego is not your true self.

Don't we all have a bit of ego in our personalities? Yes, we do. Even monks have an ego! It is just that some are better at taming it than others. Some care enough about others, and the world, to make the attempt to understand the ego. What I know for sure is that being able to get in touch with ego, understand it, and lovingly manage it is essential on a daily basis. Doing so enables us to live a life steeped in peace, generosity, service, and forgiveness, thereby creating true joy, aliveness, prosperity, abundance, and thriving!

Are you ready to sow seeds of love and to prosper beyond your wildest dreams? Your soul hopes you are feeling stirred up enough to take the next leap into your succulent life. Perhaps you already hear it whispering to you, "Come over here, darling. I am waiting." But first...

SOCIAL CONDITIONING

You might wonder: Where in the heck did ego come from to begin with? I believe we all started here on Earth with a clean slate, but even as we were being born we were being socialized into what we are not. As early as the Labor & Delivery Room, in the moment after birth, socialization begins. In the past, boy babies were placed in blue blankets, and baby girls into pink ones. Studies have shown the ways in which we communicate differently with boys and with girls and how this plays out in our social and psychological development. The color pink is seen as "softer and quieter" while blue has represented "strong and loud."

There are many ways we all have been conditioned. As we grew up, some of us were told that we were bad by nature, sinners, unworthy, not good enough, not smart enough, or not thin enough. Some were taught that boys could do math and girls could not. Others were taught that boys played sports and girls could not. Some were taught that girls were good at reading and writing while boys were not. And others were taught that boys grew up to be men to work and make money, and girls grew up to be women who had babies and spend the man's money. These are absurd ideas, of course. I am sure you can think of various ways you were socialized to think of yourself as "less than." We all were subjected to our well-meaning parents, the media, advertisers, religious authorities, teachers, and many others. I think we have all heard at some point that forgiveness is a sign of weakness or giving in to another. But that of course is not true at all.

Our parents did the best they could, given what they were taught by others. They bought into the same system as they became adults. In the past, they did the best they could with their state of consciousness, and they are doing the best they can with their current state of consciousness. We all do our best with our current state of consciousness as well—but since you have this book in your hands it means you want to grow and stretch beyond limiting beliefs.

We have also viewed social images demonstrating how women are to be viewed as sex objects. We view images that demonstrate that men are to be aggressive and domineering. We bought into the sick notions that we need more material goods to define our worth. There are messages telling us that "money is bad." There are messages that say, "greed is good." Too many times this type of messaging becomes imbedded in our consciousness. We must undo the falsities. And the time is now. When I was in elementary school, I remember seeing a poster at the local K-Mart with the picture of a Rolls Royce and a man in a tuxedo holding a martini glass, with the caption reading, "Poverty Sucks." That sent quite a message! Then there were the cigarette advertisements and commercials. I remember one commercial with a doctor in a white coat at his desk smoking a cigarette remarking that smoking is good for you! Take some time to think about those egoic social and media images and messages and how they have shaped you, your ways of thinking, and the choices you have made. Become more aware. Remain willing to notice the ways your ego may buy into social messages. When you let go of these old ways of thinking, you open yourself to more possibilities.

ALOHA EGO: THE PROCESS IN ACTION

By engaging with the Aloha Ego process, you are going to understand what it means to choose from living in hell or heaven. This is about a shift in your attitude and state of mind, which you may need to do many times each day.

There are four steps. Try to keep these in order in your mind.

To start, all you have to do is be quiet and still enough so you are aware of when your mind begins to fall into ego states such as drama (poor me!, why me?), anger, or an anxious, competitive, or unforgiving mode. That awareness of ego is the key to

EXERCISE

Think of a current issue or problem or question you might be struggling with. Now follow steps one to four below carefully.

"I have had the privilege
of losing everything."
—Byron Katie

starting to manage it. The noticing-thoughts practice you engaged in earlier on will help you with this deepening exercise.

1) Now, greet and welcome your ego by saying to yourself, "Aloha, ego, and welcome."

After you greet your ego, you can say to yourself, for example, "I notice thoughts of anger and frustration welling up in me every time after I speak with my ex-husband. I notice that my fists are balled up, my shoulders are tight, and my blood pressure is rising. I keep thinking about the day he said he wanted a divorce. That day still haunts me."

Try to be with your feelings and acknowledge whatever comes up for you. Here you have named the upset or trigger.

2) Show love to your ego by saying, "Aloha, ego. I know you are here to teach me, and for that I love you."

This time you can ask something like, "What is all of this anger and frustration here to teach me?" Now, you may feel like your soul is having a chat with your ego, which is perfect. It might reveal why you feel revengeful, jealous, hurt, or stuck in pain. You can step gracefully into asking for the gift to reveal itself in this situation. It may be hard to hear the truth. Wait patiently. Be open to hearing the truth. Be ready to be raw and honest. Try to face it, so you can move on from your conflicts and pain. This takes courage from deep within you. If need be, pray, meditate, or journal. Let the "lesson" come to you. The lesson will come. When it comes, you can say something like this to yourself, "I understand now that I am supposed to take a walk when I get upset and angry at my ex-husband. I can just take a walk to clear my mind and forgive instead of stewing around in my upset. When I do that, my blood pressure will lower and I will be more at peace. I remember we divorced because we fought all the time. We were always at odds despite our attempts to solve things. Now I have an opportunity to find out who I am in the world. I can do more of my art work, travel, and help other women who have been through this."

After you get the lesson or reason, say, "Aloha, I love you." This is how you make peace with yourself and your life. (Remember, if you are stuck and can't seem to move on from something that may be impeding your day-to-day living, seek out a qualified psychotherapist to guide you.)

Once you fully understand the lesson, it is time to release the ego's hold on you.

1) Say welcome to ego by saying to yourself, "Aloha, ego. Let's have a chat."

2) Say I love you to ego by saying to yourself, "Aloha, ego. I love you and I want to know what you are here to teach me."

3) Say good-bye to ego by saying to yourself, "Aloha, ego. Good-bye."

You can state, "Now I now release you, ego. Ta ta."

4) Now you can say, "mahalo" (thank you) for the experience.

At this point you may want to envision your ego floating away, out to sea, back into the no-thing-ness it came from. As it dissolves, you understand that your soul has shifted to the forefront. And at this point you know you can live more freely from your divinity. Go ahead and think of a current situation your ego has been working over-time in. Now re-work the steps of the Aloha Ego process with your own example.

When you take the time to be honest with yourself about the ego and its fearful, greedy, domineering ways, you can live more from your true nature. Keep in mind the four steps to the "Aloha Ego" process:

1. Aloha (Welcome).

2. Aloha (Love).

3. Aloha (Good-bye).

4. Mahalo (Thank you).

EXERCISE

State the following three times, and try to do so smiling, "Aloooooha ego, aloooooha ego, aloooooha ego." Although this is a serious exercise, I created it to have a fun way to manage daily stressors. And by all means exercise your new abilities by coming up with your own unique and entertaining ways for taming the ego.

Take in the following wise words from another great teacher, author Louise Hay. She writes,

"I remember the days when the idea of becoming your own best friend sounded like a silly motivational slogan, but now I know it's crucial that we do so. Most of us are so hard on ourselves. As I look back on my own life, I can see that for years I made the mistake of believing that I could actually motivate myself to make positive changes by beating myself up—the old 'kick in the ass' mentality. Now I see this is for what it really is—a way of reinforcing limiting beliefs that keep us frightened and stuck."

Louise's words resonate deeply with me because before I opened to my spirituality I had often tried to "drill sergeant" myself into doing things differently. But it always felt so punitive, forceful, and not in alignment with my core. I eventually realized it was my ego's way of talking, and it definitely was not motivating me. Although I did not know it at the time, what I really needed was pure loving kindness and wisdom to get me going. Thank you, Louise, for affirming the good in all of us.

EXERCISE

Honestly answer and elaborate on the following questions in your journal.

- Am I consciously in control of my daily choices and habits?
- Have I been lazy about making the right choices for myself?
- Do I deny myself healthy foods and exercise?
- Do I deny myself joy and adventure?

continued on next page

CHOICES

Do you want to make wiser choices in all areas of your life and to help heal the wounds in the larger psychic bloodstream of all living things?

The exercise below will also help you find positive ways to manage your ego's grip, to make better choices, and release old ways of thinking and viewing the world.

If you become quiet and still enough you may sense the internal struggles taking place as you contemplate each question. Allow yourself to deeply consider the questions and be compassionate with yourself as you do. Remember, we all have some ego work to do. No one is left out of this. Any sense of un-ease or anxiety you may be experiencing is actually your soul calling you to wake up and notice something or it could be that a bigger shift is needed within you. Might you even be able to see that on a grand scale it is the **larger soul consciousness** of the world, calling everyone to shift? We are all being called to evolve. You can view your impending changes from either a micro or macro perspective, or a combination thereof. I highly urge you to consider both. Remember, everything is connected. Either way those struggles are gifts for you to learn and grown from. It is the light wanting to heed the call to come forth to shine even brighter. We have work to do and we need to pay attention to these messages. We need to do the work, such as to take the next step or, depending on the situation, refrain from taking a step. When you are at a point of noticing the inner turbulence or unrest, and you can get quiet enough to be with it, you can begin to ask, **"What is my next right action?" or "What is the right thing to do?"** Trust that the answers will come.

ACHIEVEMENT

This work does not mean you cannot be goal oriented, financially successful, or wealthy in all ways. This is about the way you go about attaining success and wealth. This is about releasing victim- and fearful mentalities and opening to your inherent heroic

continued from previous page

- Do I overspend to buy material things that I think will make me feel better?
- Do I get caught up in my emotions and let the drama of the feelings overtake me?
- Do I often take things too personally and act out from fear?
- Am I living in fear?
- Do I think others are bad and that the world is a bad place?
- Am I stressed out on most days?
- Am I more often in a sad state, thinking about the past?
- Am I more often in a worrisome state, anxiously thinking about the future?
- Do I struggle against myself?
- Do I let my ego control me?
- Do I complain and gossip frequently?
- Do I often find faults with myself and others?
- Am I competitive, desiring to win at all costs?
- Am I withholding of my love?
- Am I tight fisted with my money?
- Do I find it impossible to forgive?
- Have I succumbed to my ego more often than I have been aware of?

self. This is also about letting go of thoughts and emotions as I mentioned earlier, which includes the pull of the energy on your consciousness. Only you can make this happen. When you get into a regular, daily practice of ego management, you will progress, and you will create a knowing that you have the power to take much more control over life's circumstances than you

"It takes guts to be gentle and kind."
—*The Smiths*

currently have, no matter where you are on your path at present. You begin to turn your fears into love, and **love then becomes the rocket fuel to propel you** into living full out. Know this, because you are doing the work—more success is on its way to you now. Stay open.

Lastly, when you are ready to forgive for good, you may feel your body change. You'll perhaps even experience less pain, less tightness, less soreness, less stress overall. Note your bodily sensations as you pause here. Take five to ten minutes right now to just breathe and scan from head to toe. Breathe and scan.

EXERCISE

Take a moment and reflect on your ego and what you are willing to do to free yourself from its ways. Answer these questions and write as much as you need to.

1. As a soul-centered person, committed to evolving myself, am I willing to forgive others and myself, over and over?

2. Am I willing to forgive for good, right now?"

CHAPTER 11: SOUL

If you completed the work in the previous chapters, you will likely be prepped for this chapter. Reconsider the dive from the top I mentioned earlier, or try another level up from where you are. Check in with yourself frequently about where you are with your willingness to dive into the teachings and how far you are willing to go. In this chapter you are invited to explore the soul and spirit from a number of perspectives.

Unlike the ego, the soul is kind, patient, and has positive self-esteem. It makes you feel blissed out when you are doing the things you love to do. It holds a positive regard for others and for nature. It feels at one with others, compassionate, empathetic, nurturing, and likes a good win-win. On the soulful or spiritual plane there are no competitors.

Are you willing to consider yourself living from this level of awareness in all areas of your life? What are some additional terms you can think of for your soul?

> ## EXERCISE
>
>
>
> In your journal write about what "soul" means to you.

I want to tell you how I opened myself to living from my soul. I will integrate some of the stories I've already shared. Then we will explore different ways to access soul.

As I mentioned, I lost a very dear person, a soul-sister friend, on 9-11. Due to the enormity of that loss and what was going on in my life at that time, including the shift in work and relationships, I began to open to my soul callings—the faint whispers that were fast becoming direct orders from a higher power. Something was waking within me at the core, and I could finally hear what had seemed like distant calls from an only somewhat familiar place. In hindsight I believe that my friend who died was sending me messages to wake up. (I will share more about her in a later chapter on relationships.) This was around the same time I started to practice yoga. A few years later, I began immersing myself in Unity New Thought and Buddhist teachings. I delved into the teachings of Dr. Wayne Dyer, who I credit for most of my early spiritual growth and understanding.

At that time, I also started waking up at four o'clock in the morning to pursue my own journal writing, drawing, praying, and meditating. I had endured another significant relationship loss, and that's when I went into a ten month period of contemplation and planning how my life needed to seriously shift.

I read works by spiritual masters. I listened to positive life affirming meditation CDs and read as many New Thought books as I could. I tried to read parts of the Bible as well, but I could only get so far. The right books would show up at the perfect moments, and I would devour them. I relished *A Course in Miracles*. I soaked in *The Tao Te Ching*. I would study these and many more as if I were back in graduate school. I would read them slowly and contemplatively. I would walk away from a paragraph then sit in silence, and go back and read more, then journal on the side. I would read and then turn to my art book and draw the images that were coming up for me.

Nothing had ever been so wildly exciting to me except for my adoration of Hawaii. So I began to think about how I could incorporate my love of Hawaii into my own life coaching program. It felt effortless to start drafting a workbook, so I worked on that in the wee hours.

I had finally stopped long enough to heed the messages from deep within me—what I initially called my "soul." As I continued to listen, and open more spiritually, I began to understand that this was a force saying, "Hi sweetie, come over here. Come on. Yes, that's it." I felt that "yes" in every fiber of my being. Now I am comfortable using many terms to describe my spirituality.

I also realized that the books were giving me so much of what my family could not. Even graduate school did not teach me to think on this level. The spiritual books taught me how to think from a deeper perspective, to claim my true identity in the world, how to feel, how to manage anxiety and stress, how to develop my spirituality, and how to relate to the world in healthy ways. I fell in love with the positive messages and the idea that I was still capable of creating the life I dreamed of living despite significant losses, hardships, and setbacks.

The inspiration from those ten months has never ended. I have stayed the course and I keep enjoying the ride. Now I am clear that I am living my soul purpose, and I want to serve in a capacity that helps many people heed their calling.

DIVINITY

This section is about understanding and accepting **your divine nature and your unlimited potential**: the truth of who you are. You are working towards allowing your divine seed to sprout and display its full grandeur. This is the opposite of your ego. Remember, although you have one, you are not your ego, it is an illusion brought about by social conditioning. When you get into the practice of taming your ego on a regular basis as discussed in the previous chapter, you will find that you can live more from your 'Uhane (your soul). Some call this their "God-centeredness" or their "Christ-consciousness" or their "Buddha-nature." There are many terms, so it is up to you to feel this out. If you have not defined your spiritual essence as of yet, consider the terminology that suits you best. Know that it can change for you also. Maybe you had or are having your own spiritual awakening, and the experience can help you define it for yourself. I have discovered that there are many types of spiritual experiences and people use different terms as they change and grow. A commonality with all awakening is a profound shift in identity—the sense of who or what you are in the world.

ASSESSING SPIRITUAL DEVELOPMENT

Having a sense of spirituality can accelerate one's life development. Since there are many layers and levels to spirituality, the following questions will help you

"Soul is a word that we use to describe the central or integral part of something, or its vital core. In its most profound sense, the word also describes the essence of every human being—it is that place within each of us

that is infinite, eternal, and universal. The soul is a source that gives rise to form, yet it is unknowable. It is elusive by its very nature, yet it must be nurtured and cared for."
—*Denise Linn, Soul Coach*

EXERCISE

Consider the following questions and elaborate on your answers in your journal.

1. Where are you with your spirituality and your development at this point? For example, can you define it for yourself?

2. Do you feel you have the capacity to observe yourself well enough to tame the ego?

3. Do you feel you are becoming more of a witness to your own life?

4. Are you at the point where you can know that you have a new capacity to go deeper than being a witness?

5. Do you want more warmth and intimacy with spirit?

6. Do you want a deeper experience with wisdom, love, and truth?

7. Do you want to let spirit show you or guide you?

8. How might you be relating to the idea of collective unity and beauty?

9. Can you trust in a higher intelligence where you know that everything, including ego darkness, wants to be free and liberated?

10. Can you see the potential for an inner psychological unification between ego and soul?

11. Are you open to experience a complete return to your Source?

12. Can you hold a willingness to stand up within yourself, and be open and sincere about what you find?

assess where you are with your own development. Remember there are no "right" or "wrong" answers.

Please check in with yourself. I wonder if you are feeling more connected, happier, or more on track with your life. Perhaps you are more open to trying creative things that you once loved to do or haven't tried yet. Maybe you have allowed more of life to flow, or let go of life stressors more readily? If you are feeling unsure or challenged in any way, I encourage you to step into this boldly yet gently. Remember **wherever you are is right and perfect.** Feel how your body is responding to what you have been reading about in this book. Maybe you have lowered your blood pressure, or lost a few of those extra pounds, or have had fewer headaches. Your body is giving you messages and trying to convey important things to you. Listen to it. As you proceed, remember to breathe, be still, and know—tune into that one true inner voice beneath all the mental chatter. Depending on how deep you want to go, you may even desire a complete break from the gravitational force of the ego.

SOUL AS MYSTERIOUS SOURCE

It can be challenging to define the soul. Let's try some more ways of looking at this. We have all heard of the term "soul calling" or perhaps someone has said to you, "Do some soul searching." What was your response to that? Did it at least make you stop and think?

I think the soul is a vast and mysterious Source by whatever name(s) you have for it. I equate soul

"The reason people awaken, is because they have finally stopped agreeing to things that insult their soul."

—*post on Facebook, author unknown*

to "Source," "Creator," or "God." I don't think there is only one way to get in touch with or name it. The following terms and practices will help you delve further.

MANA (LIFE FORCE)

In Hawaii, the term "mana" is used to describe life force. This force is at work in everything and everyone. I find mana in nature all around me—flowers effortlessly blossom and trees instinctively grow tall. Sand naturally shifts. The tropical breeze just blows. The tides change. Fishes and turtles just swim. Butterflies just fly. Birds simply soar. One of my very favorite creatures, the ancient-looking and "meditative" Jackson's Chameleon slowly observes and climbs. It seems to me that the same Source that aligns the planets and makes the stars shine is the same life source from which we all come.

Mana also refers to the waves of invisible energy moving and shifting in and around the universe all the time. If mana (source, spirit, energy, God, nature) created a solar system and an entire universe, then isn't it possible that it created us? Perhaps we are here as a soul living in a body, functioning from within the same energy fields as the solar system. Can you consider the universe as one large living organism and that we are each holy cells within space doing our tiny part to keep the whole of life functioning and thriving?

You will have to feel things out for yourself as to how you can have a deeply meaningful connection with the larger body of life. I am merely a guide, here to take you to your leaping off point where **you have the option to dive in deeper** and use the many tools I am offering so you can stay inspired and keep going with the flow.

WISDOM TRADITIONS

One way to get in touch with your soul is to find teachings about the soul within wisdom traditions. Wisdom traditions take more of a mystical perspective. Many great teachers have found the core commonality of "love" as the main thread within all wisdom traditions.

Here is a definition from c-c-n.org that helps explain wisdom traditions:

"Wisdom traditions are found in religion, as in the contemplative traditions of Buddhism, Christianity, Vedanta, Daoism, Sufism; and in the history of philosophy, as in the writings of Plato and Aristotle, which were Christianised in the Neo-Platonic schools in the early Church, and as such still survive today. Wisdom in this sense refers to means of personal transformation, of expanding our consciousness in the ways we understand and relate to our world. Through such practices, we may rediscover universal truths about our own identity, our potential for goodness, the nature of genuine happiness, and the role of consciousness in the universe."

Of those mentioned, which wisdom tradition might resonate most with you? Are there certain ones that you are intrigued about and would like to research more?

BODHISATTVA

Sometimes it takes a connection with a spiritual figure to help motivate you. For example, you can connect with what the Buddhists call a "bodhisattva." From Wikipedia.com,

"In Buddhism, a bodhisattva is an enlightenment (bodhi) being (sattva). Traditionally, a bodhisattva is anyone who, motivated by great compassion, has generated bodhicitta, which is a spontaneous wish to attain Buddhahood for the benefit of all sentient beings."

Many people are fond of the Chinese Goddess figure known as Quan Yin. She has been known as a compassionate rebel and often appears with a tear running down one cheek.

"As a witness, you begin to discover that you are not that which you have been observing; you are not those things that you have been noticing about your body. Instead you are the noticer."
—*Wayne Dyer*

GANESHA AND SPIRITUAL SYMBOLS

There is a lavender farm in upcountry Maui and on one of my trips there I observed a young boy curiously peering into the fish pond. Next to the pond was a beautiful cobalt blue statue of an elephant. In India, the elephant is known as Ganesha, representing the remover of obstacles. I was intrigued by the little boy's diligence, so I watched him for a while. It seemed the boy wanted very badly to stick his hand into the pond. He kept holding up his hand as if he would dive in and try to catch one of the fish. Then he would withdraw his hand, back away, and just peer in. What I really enjoyed was the way it seemed the Ganesha served to symbolically protect the fishes. I also have a Ganesha pendant I wear around my neck on days when I feel like I need some "universal assistance." From Wikipedia:

> *"Ganesha is widely revered as the remover of obstacles, the patron of arts and sciences and the deva of intellect and wisdom. As the god of beginnings, he is honoured at the start of rituals and ceremonies. Ganesha is also invoked as patron of letters and learning during writing sessions."*

If you are willing to consider Ganesha for a moment, think about if there are any obstacles preventing you from living from your soul. Might you ask Ganesha to remove them for you?

Are there spiritual symbols that particularly intrigue you, or inspire you? Many people are drawn to the Christian cross, the Egyptian Ankh, and to the Star of David. There are many more of course. I encourage you to seek out spiritual symbolism and to be open to images that represent something powerful to you. They help to keep you connected to your soul.

SOUL OF THE EARTH

For many people, connecting with nature is their "religon." They find peace in the forest or by the sea, in a seed or in a creature. Seeing the result of our poor ego choices and how the Earth is now becoming increasingly toxic, some may

"And forget not that the earth delights to feel your bare feet and the winds long to play with your hair."
—*Kahlil Gibran*

become spiritually en-livened as environmental advocates. They may create a life legacy and life purpose based on this type of personal mission.

AKUA (GOD)

In Hawaii, the word for God is "Akua." When I am living my spiritual practices, I am consciously connected to God. Akua calls to me, and I connect with Akua because I have set myself up for listening to the one true inner voice. It reminds me of my authentic power and to search my soul frequently.

There is something mysteriously powerful about consciously placing my bare feet, the soles (souls) of my feet, on the 'aina (land) in Hawaii. There is a vibrational energy getting matched up, or tuned into, the ancient and mysterious parts of me. As a result I am able to connect with God—the highest part of myself and the entire world. Reconnecting with the Earth is an activity that helps me regain my footing when I have been off course. It helps me come back to my center.

When do you feel connected to "God?" How do you connect with your "God?" Might there be a way to consciously connect through nature?

THE TAO

Ancient texts can also help you connect with your soul and spirituality. The Taoist Master Lao Tzu has much to teach about life. He was a philosopher of ancient China who authored *The Tao Te Ching*. People refer to this book as The Tao. Tao means to be in "the way." This also means to be centered or balanced. I have read a few versions of this book. Lao Tzu helps you see and experience life from a moral or spiritual perspective by offering descriptions of extremes in life. By analyzing the extremes they help us to find the middle way, the more balanced way of life. Each of the book's verses is short, so you can contemplate them

---

EXERCISE

Take some time to place your bare feet on the 'aina (earth or land) today. Dig your toes in the sand, or feel your feet walking in the yard, or the garden, or gliding through crunchy fall leaves. Let the soles (souls) of your feet connect with the aliveness of the planet. Afterwards, journal on the following questions:

1. What or who might you feel connected with?

2. Can you name it?

3. What does this experience feel like?

4. Do you feel any sense of responsibility for the planet, and in what ways might you begin to?

"The clearest way into
the Universe is through
a forest wilderness."
—*John Muir*

carefully and take away a simple message. The Tao suggests that **you have an inherent nature of knowing** what that "Source" is for you. Here is the last part of the 54th verse, from Wayne Dyer's book on the Tao, in the chapter titled, "Living as if Your Life Makes a Difference,"

"The Tao is everywhere; it has become everything. To truly see it, see it as it is. In a person, see it as a person; in a family, see it as a family; in a country, see it as a country; in the world, see it as the world."

Living in the Tao is definitely one great example of how you can practice being in the world. I choose to trust in the teachings of the Tao and have faith in the mysterious Source. It is everywhere present, including in me. I feel and know that it moves me. When I am in alignment, I remember that I came from the Source, that it walks, talks, thinks, sleeps, and dreams me. It prays me, meditates me, heals me, and works me. It writes me, reads me, and types me. I feel as if we are one and we co-create in the world. The Tao reminds me that I am the love the world needs me to be. It reminds me to keep writing the book even when I feel depleted, confused, lazy, or off track. That is what I live for every day…to be sourced like that!

EXERCISE

Journal on your connection to the earth. Ask yourself the following questions:

1. How does the earth, my home, sustain me?

2. How do I contribute to sustaining the earth?

3. What could I do better or differently to help clean up our oceans, forests, or other physical landscapes?

4. Is my soul calling me to help sustain the earth?

5. Might I be designing my life purpose around how I can better connect with and serve the planet?

6. Are there any other ideas I have for healing the planet? Explore this in your writing.

Do you want to be sourced by something greater? I am certain that you can **intimately know your reason for being and co-create your purpose every single day** with your Source. Even if you have a bad day, you can still mobilize Source.

SOURCE AS ALL GOOD

I can't tell you what to think, but I can ask you to think *about* certain things if you are open to it. If you have ever heard you are bad by nature, consider that

"Every human being's essential nature is perfect and faultless but after years of immersion in the world, we easily forget our roots and take on a counterfeit nature."

—*Lao Tzu*

you came from a beautiful Source, just as vast and mysterious as the universe. And it is all good. Consider this, if you came from a vast and good Source, then could it be that you, too, are vast and good? If Source does not condemn or judge, then could you also have potential for less self-condemnation or judgment as well? Is it possible to live less and less from your ego, to be able to **fully embrace your goodness?** Think of a time when you did something really wonderful for someone else and how you felt. Could THAT be the feeling that your Source wants you to feel more of?

As spiritual beings, energetically sourced and having a human experience, I think we are capable of radiating the highest energy frequencies available. I think Source wants us to not just believe, but to **know and act** as if we are one with it. There is no separation.

JESUS

I think Jesus expressed Source as well. Perhaps God was living through, and as, Jesus. The Bible tells us Jesus was capable of performing miracles...demonstrating the human potential for all of us.

In her book *Lessons in Truth*, Emile Cady says of Jesus,

> *"He poured forth into everyday use, among the children of men in the ordinary vocations of life, that which he received of the Father. His knowledge of spiritual Things was used constantly to uplift and to help other persons. We must do likewise, for newness of life and of revelation flows in the faster as we give out that which we have to help others."*

EXERCISE

Contemplate what it would feel like to live from your soul (or source, mana, heart, Godness, Goodness—you name it) every day. I invite you to make the choice to save yourself as if you were a drowning baby. You, your life, is a drowning baby, and only you can save you. You are worthy of this gift. Now journal your thoughts on what it means to save this drowning baby.

Can you claim such healing powers for yourself? Consider this: our bodies are miracles in that we are regenerative creatures. Just observe a scab that heals on its own. Our bodies do this many times each day. What if we are capable of much more healing and what if all we need to do is change our beliefs about the possibilities?

Can you see your body as a divine holy temple, or a holy monument? If allowed to, could Source move in and as you? Can you choose to surrender to this potential, the Christ or Buddha within? Can you tame your ego, on a daily basis, so there is more room for God, goodness, and healing potential just as Jesus did?

> "'Go preach…Heal the sick…
> freely ye have received, freely give,'
> he said." (Mt. 10:7-8, KJV)

Feel free to write down whatever feels absolutely right and true for you and use more than one term for "God" if you wish. Know that this might change for you over time.

EXERCISE

Exercise: Complete this sentence, "I (your name) choose to live from my _____.
Here are some examples: Innate Goodness, Godness, Divinity, Source, Soul, Spirit, Oneness, Mysterious Source, Loving Nature, Awakenness, Unity, Intuition, Christ-self, Buddha Nature.

ANCIENT HUNA PHILOSOPHY

In the ancient Hawaiian Huna (secret) philosophy, and in certain spiritual practices, the term "soul" takes on a bit of a different meaning. The Huna way tells us there are three selves. The Huna practice brings these three selves into a working harmony, but what I like most is that breathing is key to knowing self or soul. Here are the three selves as characterized by author Sondra Ray from her book *Pele's Wish*:

1. Unhipili, the lower self (ego mind), has the consciousness of a child and counts on the uhane (see below) for guidance, for love and caring, for stability and concern. It follows orders, and it is comparable to a servant. This is a basic self. One must love it and free it from guilt and sin.

2. Uhane, the middle self (the conscious mind, or soul), handles creative imagination and gives guidance to the lower self. It tells the lower self that it is forgiven, cleansed, and loved.

3. Aumakua, the higher self (the super conscious mind, Mother, Father, God mind), is your personal connection to a "higher source" or power.

This is known as the source of insight and inspiration, and it tells you what you can do through dreams, visions, hunches, etc. The way to contact this self is via prayers from the unhipili (the lower self or ego mind as indicated above). The knowledge of what to do to achieve a particular end and how to do it is revealed through the aumakua (the higher self or super conscious mind as noted above). Prayers for any healing must be communicated to the higher self, or nothing will happen. In these prayers, mana (vital life force) is a very high vibration.

Whether one relates to the Buddha, Jesus, Bodhisattva, the Virgin Mary, Hindu gods, Mother Earth, Akua, or all of the above, in my mind, no one is better than the other. If I were to get caught up in the kind of thinking that says there is only one way, I would find myself functioning from ego: from fear. Remember that fear creates much internal as well as external conflicts and wars. The planet does not need any more of that. Let's all raise the vibration to love frequencies by choosing differently, shall we? Your soul absolutely knows what is best.

Sam Keen, Harvard and Princeton Professor of Philosophy and Religion, tells us,

> "The great metaphors from all spiritual traditions—
> grace, liberation, being born again, awakening from
> illusions—testify that it is possible to transcend the
> conditioning of the past and do a new thing."

Also, from Keen's website:

> "Human life is a journey whose end is not in sight.
> Searching, longing and questioning is in our DNA. Who
> we are and what we will become is determined by the
> questions that animate us, and by those we refuse to ask.
> Your questions are your quest. As you ask, so shall you be."

Ensure that you have answered the questions from page 127 in this chapter. If you have given serious contemplation to each one, you probably have

"Build thee more stately
mansions, O my soul,
As the swift seasons roll!
Leave thy low-vaulted past!
Let each new temple,
nobler than the last,
Shut thee from heaven
with a dome more vast,

Till thou at length art free,
Leaving thine outgrown shell
by life's unresting sea!"
—*From "The Chambered
Nautilus" (last stanza)
by Oliver Wendell Holmes, Sr.*

a better sense of direction toward your life purpose. Remember to practice first by making simple changes. Start, for example, by taking a new route to work or brush your teeth with a different hand. Then branch out to try new things that affect how forgiving or compassionate you are. Keep changing your thoughts. Try things out and keep at it. Begin over and over.

As long as you come from the heart and **stay close to the heart** you can live your soul purpose and make significant change for the world no matter your religiosity, spirituality, or belief system. In choosing your inspiration, I invite you to always think for yourself and get away from group-think. If you buy into systems that box you in and have any sort of fear-based quality, I ask you to return to the question, "Who am I?" And **listen to your heart**. See what feels good to you. **Connect with people and places that truly help you feel good about being human in the world.**

It seems clear that **life has given us many beautiful ways to reveal love. Remember, love does not discriminate. How abundant and generous!**

CHAPTER 12: TRANSFORMATION

Earlier I mentioned that even when you are diligently working on ego management and connecting with spirit, you will be tested. This is a part of your overall practice and evolution. Stick with it, even through the hard stuff, and your consciousness will be transformed—it might even feel like a familiar return or a transformation back to your truest self.

Be on the lookout for this—you can go from feeling blissful, focused, and on track, and then someone will show up to press your buttons, or you will face a challenging circumstance and get out of alignment. People may try to trick you into thinking you are crazy, or they may even make direct statements that make you pause. Remember that this is a part of the process and practice of spiritual evolution. Life will simply continue to bring you lessons and opportunities to change. It is important to **remain awake enough to see these as lessons to learn from and move on from.** Every single lesson and encounter has the potential to teach you. They can reveal to heal. This chapter delves into how life experiences help to further open and expand your beingness.

BIOGRAPHICAL INFORMATION (BIOS)

Sharing bios can help us relate with one another, which is why I share elements of my life with you throughout this book. Bios help you see that you are not alone and that everyone suffers. They can also help remind you of how far you've come and to note your brilliance.

After my biological father died, my mother would marry again, twice. Her last marriage took us into the military world. We moved many times. I am now not at all afraid of moving boxes or of a good community-wide garage sale! I love the idea of moving on. To me it's not so much what I am leaving, but what I am gaining, exploring, and learning. I apply this principle to all areas of "moving on" in my life now. Moving so often has helped me to appreciate new experiences, new adventures, and new people. Of course, there were negative aspects to moving frequently as well, but I have come to terms with them and released them.

Have you ever experienced a big move, and how was that for you? Perhaps you had multiple changes going on at once. How did you manage that?

It was the move to Hawaii that opened my young eyes to life and to many levels of diversity. The New-Agey, earthy, and open-minded culture encouraged my intellect, my love of nature, my love of the ocean, and my desire to connect with and excel in life. I relished the generosity of spirit and the way the neighborhoods were diverse and open to all types of ethnicities and spiritual beliefs. I was fortunate to meet brilliant, creative, smart, caring friends from so many ethnic backgrounds who all helped to look out for me and inspire me. My (then) new step grandparents also helped to orient me to the island way of life. I recall many nice dinners from my grandparent's lanai (balcony or patio) surrounded by glowing tiki torches and over looking Pearl Harbor. That setting, a grand setting on Officers' Row, at the Camp Smith military installation, literally helped me view life from a larger perspective.

I've mentioned that I put myself through college, earning a B.A. in sociology from the University of North Carolina in Greensboro, and then my M.S.W. in clinical social work from Tulane University in New Orleans, Louisiana. I was active in college as a founding member of the Women's Leadership Coalition and participated in women's consciousness raising groups. I gave talks and presentations on domestic violence and negative portrayals of women in the media. I also led community Take Back the Night marches to speak out against rape and violence.

EXERCISE

Take some time to journal on the following questions:

1. Who has inspired me in my life?

2. What powerful stories or influences do I remember?

3. How were the experiences a "practice" for me?

Note your gratitude to each person and send them silent blessings after your journaling. You may even be inspired to reach out to them to state your appreciation. Just go with the flow, be creative, and ensure that you follow up.

As I indicated earlier, after graduate school, I longed to return to Hawaii. So I replanted myself on the island of Maui and served as a Clinical Social Worker working with families, and for a while I served families on the island of Lanai. I encountered remarkable kindness and hospitality from locals there. On Lanai, I was given a wonderful office at the local school and was invited into homes, to "talk story" (a type of informal chat in Hawaii). It was a way to casually gather information on the identified client or the family I was working with. I also met people from all over the world in the form of Japanese, German, French, and Australian tourists.

On those ferry rides to and from Lanai I also remember passing mysterious-looking military submarines and dozens of playful dolphins riding the wake of the ferry. In a sense, on the way to work, I got to be a tourist every day! That experience definitely helped to restore me.

Did you ever feel like you were starting all over after moving to a new place? Can you think of other new experiences that helped to shape you?

I moved to the San Francisco Bay Area in 1998 and worked with non-profit organizations performing consulting, therapy, clinical supervision, case management services, and eventually transitioned into health coaching, medical social work, and life care planning. Earlier I mentioned that I had entered a doctorate program at that time as well, but as I learned, I needed to let go of that stress and go through a "fun in the city" phase. I realized I was not enjoying the school, nor did I need any more school loan debt. Once I got clear on my direction I lovingly let go of the program and the burden of "getting another degree" to further define me. I was happy to release the idea that "another advanced degree will make me rich and a better person" noose from my life.

Maybe you have released something similar? What was it, and what was that experience like for you?

The harsh life experiences that cut me wide open ended up bringing the gifts of seeing, knowing, understanding, and navigating the world well beyond my years. You see, I now know that those experiences were meant to be. I know. I had to experience those hard times for very good reasons. In a sense, they nudged me in the right direction, and now I feel changed at the core. It took me many years, but I did my soul searching and grew to accept my own strength of character, resiliency, and unwavering positive attitude, which have all helped me to heal my wounds and end my suffering. I am still learning and evolving. As everyone does, I have bad days and stressful times, but they are far fewer. Remember that **peace and happiness are choices** that we can all make!

Knowing a thing or two about change and having overcome the odds, I am here to serve as your guide and **help you to accept uncertainty and the inevitable** in your life so you can increase joy and feel balanced.

CHANGE: THE ONLY CONSTANT

Life is change management and that means we all get plenty of practice with the only constant: change. How well you embrace change affects your experience of the revitalization journey. Your path to fulfillment will be shorter or a whole lot longer depending on whether you embrace change or fight it. You get to make that choice.

EXERCISE

Take time to journal on aspects of your life that have transformed you or you wish to transform. It might be helpful to refer back to your forgiveness script and re-scripting exercise from chapter 9.

CHANGE: TO DEEPEN SPIRITUALLY

I once taught a class at Unity of Berkeley on "Finding Yourself in Transition" based on the book by Unity Minister Robert Brummett. He is also a Buddhist practitioner. It was an honor to be asked by the retiring minister, Dr. Rev. Patricia Keel, to lead this class at a critical time for the organization. The purpose of the class was to help people understand how to embrace all kinds of change that come our way by virtue of finding, or remembering, our spiritual center. This was an opportunity for people to go deeper spiritually and to explore within themselves why some of them were having such a hard time with the minister's retirement.

Oftentimes, psychological wounds from childhood hold us back, or make us put up resistance, which is what I observed in this case. Very well-meaning individuals, and I mean some pretty evolved spiritual people, were acting out. This was not bad or wrong. They were just playing their part in the Unity "family" dynamic based on an upset to their familiar experience and resistance to change that they could not readily embrace at the time. I tried to hold their discomfort and pain in a sacred way. From the very first class, I made clear that it was not going to be a processing or clinical group whereby there would be a lot of cross sharing. Rather, per the book and the minister's suggestion, I was to lead a group in which people could face their own fears and do some deep inner work without a lot of discussion or debate as to why the minister was leaving at that time. The minister knew I could hold the group and lead it from a meditatively and authentically powerful way. But neither she nor I could predict precisely where people were at in terms of their willingness to participate in this way.

CHANGE: THE EYE OF THE STORM

I led that class to explore how we have been conditioned by society to live separate from our Source, especially when we are stressed out or upset. After the first few classes, it was revealing that some people left the group. They left the group that was going to challenge them about embracing change, remind them of their divinity, and urge them to go deep into themselves. Instead, they moved to a class next door that had just formed. The title of that class was "The Eye of the Storm." It was right and perfect for those who left my group to attend that group as it was more of an outwardly processing group. In it, they were encouraged to talk about their upset. Those who left needed to be in the eye of their own storm before they could move on to embrace the real change taking place deeper within their psyche. I affirmed for those who stayed in my group that they were ready to personally go in to themselves to process their own issues with change, and that the others were free to join any group that resonated with their soul needs. Most of those who stayed in my group were newer to Unity and they did not need to outwardly process why the minister was leaving or debate it. Several had not yet become identified as part of the Unity family and therefore did not have a need to declare their upset.

CHANGE AS "LETTING GO"

Intuitively, I took a risk as a teacher to state in advance that the nature of my group was not to outwardly process, but to go in to our inner selves, just as our spiritual practices were teaching us. I guessed this would be a turn off to some. But, this way, we avoided unnecessary drama and projection onto others. We went "in" to do our own work. Neither group was better than the other. People just had different needs at the time. But it was a good lesson for me as a group facilitator to observe the needs of the group who left and to let them go without feeling like they, or I, were bad or wrong. Essentially, they took care of themselves, and I took care of the group members who stayed. Sometime later it was conveyed back to me that the cross sharing in the other group had become become intense. I am glad I stayed true to the minister's request and to my own way of leading and honoring the purpose of the group even though the group sort of remodeled itself. I managed the change of the group in an intuitive way. As a result, I see the whole example as God's way of taking care of everyone based on their consciousness at the time.

Can you recall a "letting go" experience during a time of change? Consider what that was like for you. Did you manage it more from processing via inner awareness or from cross discussion with others? Was there drama? Was it peaceful? Either way, what was going on inside you?

DOING THE WORK

By continuing to teach classes and workshops, I continue to expand myself by learning from others. To me, it is a co-creation, a shared learning that fuels the classes. I also enjoy listening to Unity New Thought talks and participating in New Thought classes. Lately I've enjoyed the talks by Rev. David MacArthur, the lead Minister at Unity of Walnut Creek, California. I also completed a few pre-ministerial classes taught by Rev. Sheila Gautreaux at Unity of Walnut Creek, and I participated in a pre-ministers' monthly discussion group. I took

Rev. Sheila's "Advanced Prayer" class and her "The Power Within" class based on the book by Unity Minister Eric Butterworth.

Sheila's prayer class was powerful because it affirmed for me, as a trained Unity Prayer Chaplain, the energy behind all prayers. Sheila helped me see the importance of forgiving at the start of my prayers as well as to recognize that every prayer connects me to the divine energy within me.

The Power Within by Eric Butterworth is a MUST read for anyone on a serious spiritual path. The writings of the Buddhist Adyashanti, Marianne Williamson, and Unity's *Daily Word* are regular resources for me also. By continuing to invest in my practice this way, I deepen who I am, and I show up better to my clinical work, my speaking, meditation, teaching events, and relationships of all types. I hold the attitude that I "get to" stay tuned in with Source and do the work. As a result, even though I still experience stress and life challenges, I have more and more moments of luminosity that propel me further into my destiny.

How about you? Where are you on **your luminosity** scale? Check in with yourself right now and rate yourself on a scale of one to ten (one being low and ten being high). Some people will feel perfectly on track and in tune with no next steps to take at this time. Others may feel they need to take action to build some momentum. Consider what you might do to further you along your spiritual path, to help you stay tuned in. What will it take for you to up your number on the scale? Perhaps you will explore CDs, music, art, books, lectures, or your own writing?

THE INSIDE JOB

By becoming aware of your own internal processes (your inside job) of thinking, acting, reacting, choosing, doing, non-doing, understanding fears, taming ego, forgiving, and un-doing the past, you can more gracefully and confidently dance with the constant of change. When you are aware of your internal processes on a daily basis, you will begin to be transformed by the **renewing of your mind**. Remember, managing the changes of life begins in your mind. Your project management software is in your head. You are wired for this; all you have to do is **begin practicing** the process that I have outlined.

An important point to acknowledge is that you are currently figuring out how all of this works, and what doesn't work for you. You are trying out different ways of mastering your life. You are in a process and moving forward with each new thought you think, and with each choice you make. Please do not resist any aspect of life, the good or the bad. Keep your heart open and deal with events as events and not as your personal problems. Work with the events and situations. Allow the energies to move through you. Don't get caught up in them or defined by them. Keep practicing. Just breathe, relax, and release.

Earlier I mentioned that at one point in my life, I finally had had enough of living how I thought I needed to live based on outside influences. All wrapped up in ego and not in touch with my soul, I was definitely not feeling the mana (divine power) that was available. I was too closed off, in my own little ego world. I thought I absolutely had to get that doctorate degree to "become somebody" who had "authority" to write a book. To really help people and to make it in life as a success, I thought I had to become a fully licensed psychotherapist. I thought I absolutely needed a man, marriage, and a family to complete me. My finances were also out of control because I thought I needed things to define me as pretty, smart, and worthy. Ego dominated my personality, so that I had no idea who I was or how to navigate my life. At that time, I had unknowingly let ego halt my potential to renew myself. I was stuck and out of touch with my true self.

When I got serious about creating the life I dreamed of and began walking a spiritual path, I realized I must get real and tell the truth to myself. The jig was finally up. I needed to begin to make those critical choices. I consciously made some changes to make my life look and feel different. But I realized that in order for my life to actually be different on the outside, I had to "be and feel" different on the inside. As I said, all of this was really an inside job. I released the noxious ideas that someone or another advanced degree or some title was going to come save my okole (butt). I definitely stopped looking for

Prince Charming. I also stopped needing the approval of others. I got out of the group-think mentality and quit drinking the corporate Kool-Aid. One of the most essential changes that I embraced was to disconnect from people who did not have my well being at heart. I decided who was not authentic and released them from my life. My focus was on what my soul needed at that time. I enjoyed my spiritual readings. Book after book would just appear, and I would delve into each one as if I were studying for a Doctorate in Life degree. That idea really spoke to me. I was different than others and I knew it. The changes I made were essential to my growth and personal revolution; they allowed me to awaken my sleeping giant.

Stop for a moment and consider your own "inside job" and how you might be transmuting as you read through these chapters. Do you get **a sense of something changing in you**, and what is it? Might your giant be awakening? Does it need to awaken to something particular?

DO MORE OF WHAT FEELS GOOD

As I emerged with my new perspective, I began to hear my soul sing loudly and proudly. It was fun to try new and different things that made me feel great. In some areas I had to muster up a lot of courage. I cherished the idea that I was no longer running with the hoi polloi. It really helped to motivate me to write more and deepen my yoga practice and prayer. I also explored more of my own art and began walking longer distances. And there were no more "happy hours," I decided, which always felt more like "crappy hours" anyway. Cable television—disconnected.

I started to tell the truth to myself about every day, every experience, every encounter, and every thought. My current debts, I declared, would be eliminated and my finances put back in order. Whereas my work had had a clinical focus to this point, I now started to

> # EXERCISE
>
>
>
> Go ahead and write a few descriptive paragraphs of your own bio and continue to craft this as much as you feel like it. Remember to be gentle with your sleeping giant.

created a spiritually-based practice and let the clinical work become a means to consciously help others in the meantime. I changed my idea of "achievement" in life.

I let go of ridiculously wanting to be a physical athlete and embraced becoming a "spiritual athlete." I released my ego's grip that I had to travel the world just so I could brag that I'd "been there, done that." And probably most importantly, I let go of the sick notion that, to be admired, I had to buy the nicest clothes, shoes, and jewelry. When I started to open, release, and let go, life began to return me to my true nature. In that way, I felt transformed. And my journey certainly has not ended.

What similar changes have you made in your life? How did it make you feel? Do you see how your bio might be changing as a result of this sharing?

SPIRITUAL ALIGNMENT

Staying in alignment with spirit, and practicing what your soul needs you to do are paramount to living the life you dream of. Don't sit by idly and wait for something to happen to you. When you act, the universe responds and like energy attracts like energy. The more your respond to life from your true self, your problems and disturbances will lessen. You can continue to learn and transcend any inner turmoil. You can commit to peace and happiness and enjoy all parts of life! You are capable of moving into the space where you experiment with thinking and acting like you imagine God (or Buddha, Life, Nature, Intuition, The Tao, Jesus, etc....) does and you suspend your intellect.

EXERCISE

Use your own word to fill in the blank—name your source: "I am capable of moving into the space where I experiment with thinking and acting like _____ does and I suspend my intellect." Now repeat the sentence three times out loud.

RE-VISITING VALUES

Consider the following—remember the values list you made earlier on in the book? Now is the time to go back and review that list and then honestly ask yourself about what you most truly value in life. What does your soul really value? Write in your journal for at least ten minutes on this topic.

After you review the values list, go ahead and refine it. Next choose your top three and circle them. Then circle your very top choice. Keep this number one value in mind as you proceed.

"When you are an instrument of thy peace (as in the Prayer of St. Francis), you are not seeking anything, you are a peace provider. You do not seek peace by looking into the lives of others and wishing they would change so that you could become more peaceful. Rather, you bring your own sense of calm to everyone you encounter."

—*Wayne Dyer*

PEACE AS A VALUE

Getting clear about and living your values will help you know on a deeper level who you are and why you are here. I think everyone wants more peace in their lives and in the larger body of life. For example, if you value peace, then you need to consciously act and be peace. You cannot be a drama queen. You cannot overreact when you get upset and cause chaos and confusion to those around you. You need to practice peace and make choices from peace. Then the things and people around you will reflect peace back to you. If you value peace, you may want to take frequent meditative walks, learn to use positive prayer, or impart peaceful themes in your writing, art work, or in conversations with a partner. Becoming aware of how you are thinking is essential. If you value peace, and you want more of it in your life, then you need to practice peaceful thoughts morning, noon, and night. You might want to create affirmations focused on peace. If you are a musician, you could play peaceful music or write a song about creating a peaceful planet. If you are a nurse or a doctor or another type of healing professional, you might want to take care to speak kindly to your patients even if you think they are being difficult or seem to be "non-compliant." I especially invite clinically trained people to impart a heart-centered presence within their patient relationships. Perhaps even consider some "out of the box" prescriptions such as meditation, volunteering, gestures of gratitude, walks in nature, finding one's life purpose, or forgiveness.

ATTITUDE

Your kulana (attitude) about changes taking place in your life is something you can choose. It took a while for this type of thinking to settle into my bones. As you know, I had to make a conscious choice to immerse myself into the study of New Thought and Buddhist teachings to begin making lasting and significant changes. With my attitude adjustment, I let go of sarcasm and condescending remarks and decided to compliment others more frequently, which felt very good.

The way you feel every day is your choice. Your rate of personal transformation is your choice. You make a choice about how you interact with people and respond to situations. You need to take control of what you think about and how you express yourself. You need to surrender to your "I AM" presence—that presence that is the noticer of the thoughts.

Your "I AM" presence is your most authentically powerful spiritual self, which you are getting back to. You will glisten and glow when you embody this presence. In essence this is an **accepting of a return to the peace and love that you already are**. If you sincerely desire it, you will return home and your return will be a sweet memory that you will notice was there all along. Softly, I urge you to **stay open to your heart-based homecoming**.

"If you are yourself
at peace, then there
is at least some peace
in the world. Then
share your peace with
everyone, and everyone
will be at peace."
—*Thomas Merton*

"The soul moves through life with grace. The ego moves through life with recklessness, chaos, and drama. The soul feels good about who it is and what it wants and needs to sustain itself, to grow and evolve. The ego never has enough; it can never leave well enough alone or see beyond

the current circumstances. It is entitled, confused, and feels stuck. The ego tirelessly swims against the current, while the soul sits back and floats in the direction that life is moving in. You're either being guided by your soul or driven by your ego. At any time, you have access to either of these realities..."
—*Debbie Ford*

CHAPTER 13: SOUL CALLING

You have been exploring and opening to soul in various forms. In this chapter, I will introduce you to a spiritual practice that your soul is calling you to engage in. I will also encourage you to make your physical health a priority. The goal here is to help you **remain focused and healthy**. Let your entire **lifestyle** (body, mind, and soul) become your treatment protocol—*the* **Rx** of your total health. Soon you will be able to integrate your soul calling with your life purpose exercises that you have been working on.

After many years of trial and error, I'm blessed to say I feel focused and on track with the life I am meant to be living. I like to see and live life from a holistic perspective. As an evolving coach, I nurture my soul in many ways, such as with painting and cooking. And the primary physical exercises that I enjoy are walking and yoga. You must integrate your body into your spiritual practices for it is the vessel, the physical home, in which your practice takes place. Loving your body is a part of this practice. Notice I did not say "obsessing" about your body. Nor did I say that your body must be "perfect." Let those social messages fade out. Open to nurturing and caring for your body just as it is.

> ## EXERCISE
>
>
>
> Answer the following questions in your journal.
>
> 1. What do I absolutely love to do?
> 2. What makes me feel great?
> 3. What blisses me out?
> 4. What lights me up at the core of my being?

GO-TO ACTIVITY

Do you have a creative or physical outlet that allows you to have fun as well as to feel healthy and totally alive? I feel strongly that everyone needs a "go-to" activity of some type which could include a form of exercise or movement. This is an activity that really nurtures you. It is not an activity that feels like work or something someone else wants you to do or thinks you should do. Give yourself permission to take any "shoulds" out of the equation right now. It is simply about **what you love to do.** To have something healthy to immerse yourself in, something you love to do, is not only going to help you align with your Source, it will also help you when you are up against life stressors and challenges.

This section can tie back into the strengths or values you listed earlier on as well. If need be, go back to your strengths and values lists and review them or refine them.

Oftentimes your values and strengths will reflect some aspect of your go-to activity. Your answers might involve something you enjoyed as a kid. Maybe it was something you loved to do, but at some point someone told you to "get serious" and you therefore stopped it completely. Maybe it is a long lost sport, a hobby, volunteering, or some interest like gardening? Maybe you enjoy chanting, singing, hiking, baking, playing guitar, dancing, looking for seashells, or biking. Perhaps you enjoy cooking, painting, reading, drawing, or something else totally unique.

Now, **commit to engaging, or re-engaging,** with this more frequently, and at least once this week. State three times, "I soulfully and whole heartedly commit to (blank) at least once by the end of this week." Now, go put this labor of liveliness on your calendar for every day you are committing to this week and ensure you follow through. Then tell a friend you trust to hold you accountable. Ask that friend to check back in with you on the day after you are slated to do it. If you already do this particular activity, commit to doing it a few more times or in a new way.

EXERCISE

Consider this: Imagine you have no one, no parent, no spouse, no sibling, no media, no schools, no teachers, no colleges, no diplomas, and no degrees that have any influence on your decision. All you have to do is consider what makes you feel absolutely terrific and alive. Close your eyes and envision yourself fully immersed in this activity. Take a few moments right now to feel into every aspect of this activity with your imagination.

BASIC HEALTH

You have heard from many sources how important it is to take care of your health, and now I am going to try to respectfully and warmly reinforce it for you. Practicing basic health helps me treat my body as a sacred temple, therefore keeping me more centered in general and motivated toward my go-to activity—mainly yoga. I practice gentle yoga three to five times per week. I also love walking long distances and entering half marathons a few times each year to keep me moving, as a way to manage stress, and to feel great. As a health care professional, I receive updated information that helps people stay aware of their health care choices. They serve as gentle reminders to me about my own practices. These are, essentially, the basics of my wellness practice. I encourage you create one too.

Following are twenty healthy practices that I recommended for anyone. If you have a serious health condition, however, please speak with your doctor.

TWENTY HEALTHY PRACTICES

1. Get at least thirty minutes of cardio exercise at least three times per week. Increase your time and distance according to your fitness level. Walking is perfectly fine. Having a dedicated walking partner helps. Take family fun walks and take note of the small and larger aspects of nature around you.

2. Get plenty of rest—eight to nine hours per night is good.

3. Drink plenty of water.

4. Eat green leafy vegetables and many types and colors of vegetables. Fill most of your plate with veggies. Buy organic if you can afford it.

5. Eat a proper serving of fruits depending on your sugar levels.

6. Eat smaller amounts of protein, especially meats. Add more fish to your meals. Eat grass fed beef if you eat meat. Eat wild caught fish when you can. But think sustainability. Eat organic free range eggs.

7. Chew slowly. Enjoy tasting your foods.

8. Shop for and prepare your meals from the framework of "spiritual energy."

9. Stop to note your gratitude for the meal, and all aspects of the meal itself such as that it came from a farmer who planted seeds, harvested the crop, and drove the tractor. You can use a moment of silence or a short prayer to thank everyone and everything involved with your food.

10. Watch your portions.

11. Educate yourself about body alkalinity. You want to balance your body pH levels and boost your immune system.

12. Look for non Genetically Modified (non-GMO) foods. Read and study labels. Something marked "natural" is not always healthy for you.

13. Enjoy your local farmers markets.

14. Eat enough fibrous foods, and take probiotics to ensure a healthy gut.

15. Cook more. Eat out less.Make healthy at-home eating fun.

16. Ask your doctor for updated blood work. Be aware of your Hemoglobin A1-C to check your blood sugar levels. Ask for a Fasting Blood Glucose test to determine your most recent sugar levels. Adjust your diet based on the results of the tests.

17. Try to make green smoothies as a way to get your greens. Here is one easy recipe: 2 cups spinach or kale, ¼ cup carrot, 1 celery stalk, ½ cup strawberries, ½ banana, ½ cup pineapple, 1 small container of lemon yogurt. Fill your blender half way with water. Blend and enjoy.

18. Stretch or do gentle yoga a few times each day and after long workouts.

19. Practice conscious breathing throughout the day. Your cells want oxygen.

20. Think of maintaining your health as fun!

MOVEMENT

If you do not have a favorite go-to physical exercise, start exploring and try-ing different things. Hiking is a healthy activity. Get out there, move that beautiful body, feel the breeze, and notice how lovely nature is. Try Stand Up Paddle Boarding (SUP) if you live near a lake or the ocean. Explore your local parks. Plan a camping trip. Sign up for a 5K or a half marathon—they often come with excellent training programs. Try daily walks, dance class, Zumba, Tai Chi, swimming, martial arts, rowing, canoeing, surfing, or free weights. Join a gym, do floor exercises—anything that floats your boat. Just get going and keep trying things that sound interesting or fun to you. With some effort and trying things out your regular go-to activity will reveal itself.

Now here are five habits to stop or seriously cut back on:

1. If you smoke, please stop. Period. Smoking is hazardous to your health. You know this. Smoking is a serious addiction. Addictions are learned behaviors. You can un-learn what you have learned, if you are willing. To stop smoking all you have to do to quit smoking is to not put cigarettes in your mouth. Many people seek out smoking cessation programs to help them. Get counseling. Try hypnotherapy. Keep trying. Join a group that allows you to examine your real issues that underlie the smoking. Try psychotherapy. Address the addiction once and for all!

2. Eliminate soda. There is not one bit of nutrient in soda. Even diet soda.

3. Seriously cut back on all sugars. Remember that carbohydrates convert to sugars so that means watch your intake levels of pasta, bread, cracker, sweets, and so on. Educate yourself about this.

4. Seriously cut back on alcohol or eliminate it altogether.

5. Seriously cut back on fried foods or eliminate them.

Overall, I urge you to start making small changes if you do not currently watch what you eat and move your body regularly. Educate yourself about ways to stay motivated. Educate yourself about healthy foods, healthy cooking, and exercise. You deserve to make this a priority. And it is never, ever too late. There is no room for excuses on this. Remember you can Google "how to" anything!

CREATING HABIT

Ideally, you want to engage in your state of being active and healthy (or with the creation of any new habit) for at least twenty one days for it to become ingrained as a way of life. The time frame is also perfect for any exercise, diet, meditation, prayer, or anything else you want to make a part of your rejuvenated life. So, if you are up for a bigger challenge, go ahead and put a health care goal on your calendar for at least one month. By doing so, you are setting the intention, making the plan, and committing to it. **Set yourself up for success**. For example, if you are going to walk or jog thirty minutes every morning for thirty days, you need to place your tennis shoes by the door each night before. Place a fresh pair of socks on top of your shoes and make it a nightly ritual. Put your running clothes in a good location also. Then go ahead and set the alarm on your phone or your clock and start tomorrow. No matter what you choose, just think it through, make a ritual, make a list, post sticky notes if you need to. And try to have some fun as you are thinking about every step of your planning. Now, tell yourself you are going to get going on this and stay committed. Try to **see the thing(s) you love to do in life as essential to living**.

Fill in the blank with the activity: "_____ is essential to my spiritual and overall healthy life."

After you partake in your activity, journal about what it feels like to reconnect with or to engage in it. You can also repeat it to yourself as a mantra.

As I mentioned, I am a strong advocate of yoga, no matter one's body type, level of athleticism, or flexibility. Yoga is a healthy practice that can help strengthen and stretch the body, mind, and soul. It can help to relax and to focus. I love how yoga teachers remind us to be non-judgmental with ourselves and others as we practice. Another thing I love is that yoga is not about competition with either oneself or others.

When I first started life coaching, I had a vision that I would be teaching classes from a yoga mat, which is what I did for the first few years. We moved our bodies according to the themes on which I focused the coaching. If we were working on opening our hearts in relationships, I would have the class open their arms wide so their chests and hearts expanded. If we were working on getting grounded with our breathing, we would engage in sitting poses and envision our roots planted into the earth. One fun yoga pose is the Lion pose. In this pose participants kneel and place their outstretched hands on their knees. I ask them to open their hearts by lifting their chests, then with wide eyes, make a huge lion breathing "roar," exhaling out negative energies. We do this three times in a row and it always generates laughter and relaxation.

If you wish to try some simple, gentle yoga right now, I invite you to read through this once, then try it. Stand up, take a few breaths, and start to tune into your body. You know your body best so if anything feels painful or uncomfortable, stop. You may want to back off and then slowly try again. Tune in to your bodily sensations. Take three deep breaths. Place your feet about hip width apart. Bring your palms in prayer position to your heart center. Now raise your arms up and over your head. Reach the tips of your fingers to the sky, stretching up, and feel your feet grounded into the Earth. Breathe. Feel opposing forces here. You are reaching up and at the same time grounding down. All four corners of the feet should remain on the floor. Breathe. Engage your leg muscles. Tuck your chin in slightly. Release your shoulders. Tuck in your belly and breathe in three deep breaths, in through your nose and out through your mouth. Bring your arms down by your side and stretch your arms down with fingers outstretched. Your core is still engaged. Your legs are still engaged. Bring your hands in front of your heart into a prayer position. Breathe. Repeat this exercise as much as is comfortable for you.

Claiming and owning your healthy activity, whatever you choose, will help you forge a path of being your own professional life coach daily—at the same time you invite your soul to be free.

EXERCISE

Affirm aloud three times, "I am like the tall, strong, and flexible Hawaiian coconut trees…firmly rooted yet expanding ever so high. I am firmly rooted, I stand tall and I live my highest self."

When you are consistent with your practice, you will possibly meet people who share that interest. You will be surrounding yourself with like-minded individuals who will continue to inspire you. By consciously choosing to get into the flow with them, you will also have to make choices about getting away from those who are energy drainers.

ENERGY DRAINERS

You've done some work on setting boundaries earlier. And those lessons can be applied here as well. It is important to think through who typically drains you of your precious life energy. As you go through your week, ask yourself the following question about people in your life.

1.   Who is truly helpful to me? Who inspires me to be my greatest?

2.   Who do I feel great around? Contemplate this, focusing on people you encounter from work and home, and any activities in between.

When you consider the people you are connecting with, stop to note how your body feels when you are in their presence. See if you tense up in an area of your body around certain people. Try to take an honest inventory of those who zap you of your divinity.

To stay in the zone of higher consciousness and healthy living, it is essential to make choices about who you will include in your life and those you don't want to include. Remember to draw healthy boundaries around those who do not support your new ways of living. Practice saying "no" in a kind yet courageous way. Other energy drainers include the television and alcohol consumption.

EXERCISE

For at least one week commit to not watching television and not drinking any alcohol. If you want the greater challenge, go ahead and commit to this for one month.

CHAPTER 14: RELATIONSHIPS

Relationships come in many forms. Even though I was a shy only child, and spent a lot of time playing alone, I had a few friends among whom I was a leader. I was a "Creative Director" with them since I loved to coordinate, teach, and direct jazz dance performances. But most of the time I was in my room, practicing dance routines and imagining dance routines. I had a relationship with those routines; they provided me a way to entertain myself when I was alone. My mind has always been one of my best friends. As a result of all my imaginings and my introspection, I have honed my visualizing skills. As a child, I also loved to teach to a classroom, the students being my stuffed animals and Barbie dolls. There was the pink fluffy mouse, the Raggedy Ann doll, Little Red Riding Hood, all three of the Charlie's Angels Barbies, and regular Barbie. I taught to my "students," often reading out loud and practicing my enunciation without the Southern twang. It felt as if I could command any audience with my confidence and my articulation. This early free play has contributed to my love of speaking, teaching, and relating with audiences today.

As I grew older, I experienced setbacks with my confidence and my ability to interact in larger social settings. But I used my ability to observe others,and I just kept trying even when it felt awkward. When we moved to Hawaii I began to open up more and to socialize in new ways. It was easier to me in a laid back culture and being around such kind people. I met friends who were leaders to me by showing me beautiful places and introducing me to beach activities and "cool" people.

As I shared earlier, Christine Snyder was one of my closest friends. We both lived in Kailua, on Oahu. We shared many fun times as teenagers playing on

Kailua and Lanikai beaches, chasing surfer boys, and dancing to music by Madonna. It was the 1980s and Christine taught me how to wear rainbow colored eye shadow, big one-sided pony tail hair, hip Hawaiian Island Creations (H.I.C.) T-shirts with cute mini-skirts, and brightly colored flat Jelly shoes. She helped me to connect with many people as she set an example of how to be social and to enjoy island life. After high school we lost touch for a while but when we did see each other, it was like no time had passed. And we eventually reconnected in meaningful ways. We enjoyed our high school reunions together reminiscing, sharing our respective life updates, and a lot of laughter. She was a true soul sister and I will never forget her commitment to me as a dear friend when I needed to reach out to her and share something important about my life. She always picked up the phone, and she always responded with care and wisdom, imparting courage and strength. I still have pages of type written letters that she sent to me when I was struggling with relationships and financial woes. I can look back and see how much sisterly sweetness and direct advice she conveyed to me.

In this chapter, I will touch on several important aspects of relationships, with Ohana (family,) friends, and teachers who are dear to me. They have all helped me in one way or another. For me, there is no topic of greater importance in life (including our relationships to our thinking, breathing, health, family, community, work, money, animals, and the planet). We can do a lot of our own inner work, but we also need one another. Together, we can co-create more greatness for each other and for the world. Remember, individual responsibility *plus* social responsibility equals consciousness.

You evaluated various life domains back in Chapter 7. There you had a chance to determine where you could take steps to create healthy change. Here you are going to focus on relationships with people.

You are naturally inter-connected with all of life. Since you are a part of the cosmic organism of life, what you do, how you think, your choices, your behaviors, all of it has a larger impact on society and the entire globe. Let's look at how relations with one another can be launching pads for a greater level of consciousness.

PEOPLE

Your relationships with people are the forums that give you repeated opportunities to grow, learn, and evolve. Yes, even the jerk, the narcissist, the macho man, the whiner, the jock, the needy one, moms, dads, grandparents, children, bosses, cousins, neighbors, distant relatives, and even the clerk at the corner store…all are here to teach you and to help raise you to your full potential.

You get to either learn to be with people, or you can learn to distance from or fully release someone if you need to. Either way, you can confront relationship change from a place of love, compassion, gratitude, and for the greater good of all.

I once had to let go of a close relationship with a good person who I thought I was going to marry, but we both decided to "lovingly release it." It was difficult and there were tears, but we let go with great respect and consciousness for one another. It was the healthiest break up I ever had. Prior to that, and prior to my spiritual opening, I would have been caught up in the "poor me, relationships define me" drama mode. Thankfully I have evolved way past that period in my life.

Can you think of times in your life when you handled a tough relationship issue from a place of drama? Can you think of a time when you handled it more confidently and from love? Which do you want more of in your life?

NON-VIOLENT COMMUNICATIONS

The Non-Violent Communications (NVC) teachings can help you understand the importance of compassionate communications in your relationships. Here is the definition of NVC as excerpted from the website, nvc.org,

> "NVC begins by assuming that we are all compassionate
> by nature and that violent strategies—whether verbal or
> physical—are learned behaviors taught and supported by the
> prevailing culture. NVC also assumes that we all share the same,

basic human needs, and that each of our actions are a strategy to
meet one or more of these needs. People who practice NVC have
found greater authenticity in their communication, increased
understanding, deepening connection and conflict resolution."

KULEANA (SACRED RESPONSIBILITY)

A Course in Miracles (a book that psycho-spiritually interprets the Bible) notes relationships as "Holy Encounters," similar to Kuleana (sacred responsibility). Imagine if we could all remember to honor every relationship or encounter in this way; we would be elevating humanity to its fullest potential. What a simple and radical concept.

How might your relationships be enhanced if you practiced NVC? Do you think it is possible to at least try to honor every relationship as Kuleana? Are you willing to remember and try this practice as much as you can? Do you want to remember this for others? Do you want others to remember this for you in your presence? I believe that most people would answer "yes" to this. Who doesn't want someone to be a fully listening heart presence when we are upset, in fear, confused, misunderstood, or in pain?

As we hold sacred space with our listening and our communication, we become more in tune with our oneness and begin to see where we can adjust ourselves to enhance love and connection. We can hold each other accountable to the truth and to transparency.

This does not mean you should let people take advantage of you or stay in an unhealthy relationship that does not meet your needs. Remember there is a healthy way to say "no" and create smart boundaries also.

A teacher about relationships I admire is author Gary Zukav. What I learned from Mr. Zukav's books is that for any type of relationship, our highest

---

EXERCISE

Answer the following questions in your journal and write as much as you feel you need to.

1. Do you think your current relationships are steeped in authentic love and connection or are they more about a "providing," as Zukav describes?

2. Where might your ego be tripped up about relationships and what work might you need to do to address this? List your action steps and begin taking action.

commitment should be to our own spiritual growth. And in a partnership, our goal for one another is to create our own authentic power. We can be a sacred presence for one another, allowing space for this potential. Zukav teaches that we are evolving past the need for just emotional holding of one another and beyond the need for relationships based on "providing" for material and emotional needs. Zukav urges us to tap deeper into the ability we all have to function more from our intuition, or God consciousness. When I read his book *Creating Authentic Powerful Spiritual Partnerships*, I knew we were in alignment with how we want to live in the world and with what we want to teach in the world.

ESSENTIAL SPIRITUAL RELATIONSHIP PRACTICE

I learned the following relationship practice from the Vietnamese Buddhist monk Thich Nhat Hanh. He says we can remember four important things when we are in distress or when another is upset. With these statements we can convey our true concern for one another. They are simple but they work. They force us to become fully present and tuned in to our needs or someone else's needs—allowing for much needed loving presence in our over-stressed and over-rushed world. We can state the following, as appropriate:

1. Darling, I am here for you.

2. Darling, I know you are there.

3. Darling, I know you suffer and that is why I am here.

4. Darling, I suffer, please help me.

RELATIONSHIP LOSS

I'd like to share a few poignant examples of loss. As I've mentioned a few times, Christine Snyder was one of my best friends. Sadly, she perished in the attack on 9-11. I'd like to tell you a story about the last time I saw Chris. Here is an excerpt from one of my newsletters.

> *Chris and I grew up together on Oahu in Hawaii. She was a wonderful person. We often laughed big, roaring laughs where we*

would be doubled over holding our bellies as we recalled high school shenanigans. Chris knew how to live and she gave from her heart and soul to others. As an arborist she was passionate about preserving Hawaiian trees and land, and she was a positive person. She was a beautiful and bright woman who continues to be missed by many. And Chris was a presence, not only with her beauty—her long legs, green eyes, and sun kissed skin. She was also smart and confident. I admired every bit of her.

A month before 9-11, I took an impromptu trip to meet up with a San Francisco friend in Maui. I had been laid off from work, and I had no business spending money on this trip, but Chris convinced me to go. She always had great ways of telling me to "get going" when I was unsure about something. She had her way of expressing a "kind confidence" that I listened to on more than one occasion. She said that she would meet me at the Honolulu airport on my layover to Maui. That was about a thirty minute drive across the island for her. I packed my bags and off I went. As agreed, Chris met me and greeted me with a fragrant plumeria lei and her beautiful smile. We sat at the airport gate waiting for my next flight as she showed me her wedding album, and we reminisced about the fifteen year high school reunion that we both had attended. We sat and visited for a few hours. She waited until my flight was called and we said our Alohas. Then she said to me, "Call me before you leave Maui. Maybe I can meet you again on your layover on the way out?" I agreed. Then off I went and spent a nice week playing in Maui.

The day of my return, I phoned Chris on my way to the Kahului, Maui airport as she suggested. She had plans to go to a yoga class that night, but she said, "Oh hell, Missy, you never know if we're going to see each other again." I thought that was an odd comment but I quickly agreed to meet up with her again at the Honolulu airport for another layover. She said, "This time, I will come whisk you away from the airport and we will go to Sam Choy's restaurant for dinner."

I was so happy that we would get to spend some more time together and I could tell her about my Maui adventures.

As promised, Chris whisked by to pick me up and away we drove to get "ono grinds" (good local food) at Sam Choy's restaurant near the airport. We had a fabulous time as I told her of my Maui activities and the new job that I would be returning to in San Francisco. She was thrilled for me, and I was equally thrilled for her upcoming trip to Washington, D.C., for a conference. She said, "If I can, I will come back through San Francisco to see you." We were both delighted at this possibility. We finished our dinner and she drove me to the airport. She got out of the car and walked around to give me one of her big, warm hugs, and we told each other how special it was to spend the time together. Chris had always been an anchor to my soul, and this time would turn out to be more precious than ever.

We said our final Alohas (a few times) then I pulled my luggage around to head off. As I stood in the baggage check line an odd feeling overcame me. I thought, "What if I never see Chris again like she said?" Then I said to myself, "Well that is an awful thought, we just had a great time, so let it go." And I did, until a month or so later when I got the news.

I returned to San Francisco and prepared to start my new job. Chris and I exchanged a few emails and she mentioned she would let me know if she could change her flight on the way back from D.C. but she wasn't confident about the possibility.

On the morning of 9-11 another friend called to say, "Wake up and turn on your television. There is some kind of terrorist attack in New York!" I watched the news in horror with the world as the Twin Towers tumbled down over and over again. I sat in my apartment trying to make sense of the disturbing news. As I walked the streets of my neighborhood I felt sadness and a deep connection to everyone.

A few days later a mutual friend from Hawaii phoned me and said, "Christine was on that plane."

I said, "What plane?"

She said, "Pittsburgh, flight 93."

We talked for a short while. Shocked, I hung up the phone and cried and cried. Chris was headed to D.C. and that was the plane diverted by terrorists. I called my mother and kept saying to her in shock and disbelief, "Chris? Christine Snyder? Christine? Christine is gone?" I told my mom over and over, "I just can't believe that Christine is gone." My mom comforted me and cried with me. She of course remembered Chris as one of my dearest friends.

I knew the stages of grief very well. I allowed myself to feel the pain, the catastrophic loss, the horror of it all. I still miss Chris, as many people do. I know for sure that her soul lives on! I can still feel the goodness in our shared laughter…sweet music to my soul. Chris and I were meant to see each other on that impromptu trip that at the time did not make any sense for me. But she was on to something with her comment about "not seeing each other again." Did she sense something? I am inclined to think she was listening to her inner voice. I will never know for sure, but something, a force bigger than either of us, knew that we needed to see each other a few more times. I love to remember her kind assertiveness by telling me to "get going." Thank God I listened.

9-11 HEALING FOR ALL

The terrible events of 9-11 helped me to wake up to appreciate all of my relationships and my relationship with my whole life. By now, we all have heard stories where the tragedies of that day have helped others find deeper meaning as well.

I continue to ponder both the insanity and the unlikely gifts of 9-11, though it is hard. It seems we must seek those gifts no matter how difficult and how dark the night. The spiritual part of me feels that those responsible for the 9-11 attacks were out of touch with their heart and souls. Part of my forgiveness and healing has been from being able to reflect on the fact that they were somebody's baby once. They were a mother and father's son. They were

"Make your next words to someone, friend or foe, worthy of being your last. We have the ability to define who we are, and our legacy with each interaction. Show empathy. Take the high road. And think before being hurtful. And always, always convey aloha."

—*From Rule #84 of a Happy Life by Clarke Graves*

perhaps a father, a brother, a husband. They were also misguided, misled, and misaligned people living in society doing the best they knew how at the time.

So what can we possibly do about the misguided ones? I think we can help raise the consciousness on the planet by starting with our own individual changes. We commit to that change and serve the world from a deeply loving place. We begin to live from love for all. And part of that is to forgive.

EXERCISE

How has 9-11 changed you, your life, or the way you look at things? How might it have affected your relationships?

As you know by now, I believe we all can be brave enough to not be bound to fears, terror, or to wage wars of any kind. Those outward wars represent the inward wars we wage on ourselves. If you haven't done so, I invite you to begin your own 9-11 forgiveness "project."

This may be a huge challenge, but if you are willing, go ahead and write out your un-forgiveness story of 9-11, and then write out your forgiveness re-script, noting the gifts—even within the pain and loss just as you did in Chapter 9 where we discussed forgiveness. Remember forgiveness is a process and it can free you.

So what is my purpose for sharing this 9-11 grief and loss story with you in a book devoted to life and living? The main reason is to help you know that **since love is eternal, death need not be viewed as fearful**—as taught to me by Dr. Jampolsky. I also share this to reiterate how short and how precious life is. Lastly, I share it as a motivator, to **help get you going** with the life you truly desire. I am certain this is what my dear friend Christine would want for us.

As you are aware from my teaching earlier in the book, it is healthy to take the time to ponder your relationship to the mystery of death itself, to befriend it, and to embrace the mystery of life and live it with purpose.

Do you believe that all of your relationships deserve this level of consideration? What are you being inspired to do for your relationships in this moment?

I invite you to **speak the words of love** your children want to hear. Tell your parents, your spouse, partner, siblings, and anyone you love how much they mean to you. Today, go tell at least three people today how much you love them.

Tad Toomay is another friend who passed away a few years ago. He was only sixty years old and died from colon cancer. He was well known and loved within the Unity of Berkeley community where I was an active member. Tad often played music with his band during the Sunday services. He was a fine musician, writer, and teacher. Below is a prayer I wrote and delivered to the Unity congregation in memory of Tad.

Let us pray.

Divine Presence, as we fall into conscious connection in this now moment, we bring to mind our beloved brother, Tad.

We affirm the great mysteries of life, and death, and the eternal Tao.

We allow ourselves to feel every step of the way...

And as we grieve the loss of our brother, each in our own unique way, we allow the waves of emotion to carry us, from shock, to denial, to confusion, to anger, to bargaining, to sadness, wherever the feeling takes us, we feel into them, good and bad.

We ebb and flow with each passing moment here at Unity, in oneness, as we move through this profound loss, this tidal wave of change in our spiritual community.

Take three deep breaths.

Now I invite you to bring our brother's face into your mind's eye.

Look into his eyes deeper, and deeper.

Now see him as if he is a baby, then a boy, a teenager, young man, and as an adult.

We note his ability to play music, gifting us with his beautiful songs.

We note his ability to be fully present, mindful, with witty humor, wisdom, that bright smile, his awareness, his generosity, and kindness.

We note Tad's sacred love for his soul mate, Mindy.

We feel into the essence of his spirit, right here, and right now.

We affirm that since love is eternal, death need not be viewed as fearful.

We see and know healing for all of his family and friends.

We affirm the following words, written and sung by Tad.

"With the sky in my lungs—And the sea in my veins—I am a part of the wonder—I am the wind and the Earth, and the sea and the rain."

So we sing and dance with the mystery of life and death, just as our brother Tad would have us do.

We affirm the healing in process, and awakening for all.

Thank you, thank you, thank you, Mother, Father, God.

And so it is. —Amen

EXERCISE

Affirm three times aloud, "It is my kule-ana (sacred responsibility) to maintain *all* relationships from my *highest* self."

I can say that both Christine and Tad lived their lives on purpose and with passion. Remember that death is life's change agent. I want you to live literally as if you were dying—dying to get up and connect with your life purpose; dying to laugh, love, and to be compassionate for others; dying to wake up each day with the goal of being a little better than you were yesterday; dying to know every relationship is a precious and sacred jewel to behold!

"The boy reached through to the Soul of the World, and saw that it was a part of the Soul of God. And he saw that the Soul of God was his own soul. And that he, a boy, could perform miracles."
—*From* The Alchemist, *by Paulo Coelho*

CHAPTER 15: PRESSED DOWN

In chapter 10, you were introduced to the Aloha Ego practice. The next few chapters are also about learning to **tame the ego** so you can manage stress and maintain greater peace. At times everyone feels at least a little pressed by life or jerked around by others. But the goal in this chapter, and in the next few chapters, is to help you to meet every pressing experience from a deeper, more peaceful place by changing the way you think about them.

Early Hawaiians knew what it means to be pressed down. They lost everything, but pressed on with the struggle for their rights. From Wikipedia, "The overthrow of the Kingdom of Hawaii refers to a coup d'état on January 17, 1893, in which anti-monarchical insurgents within the Kingdom of Hawaii, composed largely of United States citizens, engineered the overthrow of its native monarch, Queen Lili'uokalani. Hawaii was initially reconstituted as an independent republic, but the ultimate goal of the revolutionaries was the annexation of the islands to the United States, which was finally accomplished in 1898." Locals would suffer the loss of their native leadership, lands, and identity. But they would persist, and to this day there are growing groups of strong advocates for native Hawaiian rights.

Throughout history Hawaiians have perservered and healed their wounds. One practice, "oki," is a way of severing problems with people or patterns of the past. They energetically "cut the cords" of those people and situations by imaging a new pattern.

You can cut the past, and create new patterns or habits in many ways. You can visualize new outcomes and shift your mindset many times each day.

"The body is a house
for the thoughts."
—*Mary Kawena Pukui*

YOU GET TO GO THROUGH

Even when you are in the "zone," living in alignment with your Source, you may be thrown off kilter as you are challenged by a new situation. Or someone might push your buttons. The goal here is to help you recognize that going through these things is a part of your spiritual evolution and that you can choose to say "aloha" to these incidents more freely. Continue opening up to God and further edge out the ego. Remember that to free yourself from the pain of psychological injury, you must start to see such experiences as energy moving through your heart and before the mind's-eye of your consciousness. You don't want to dam up the process by resisting. Don't ask, "How can I fix this?" Instead, return to asking, "What part of me is being upset by this?" Take some time to observe where you may feel vulnerable. That will help you return to your true self, your spirit—God within. Be present to any tightness or tension that might ride along with that pain. Go deeper, stay calm, remain open, and let it go. The relaxing into the experience allows the release.

I once attended a spiritual training for ministers, practicioners, and prayer chaplains in Oakland, California, led by Reverend Michael Bernard Beckwith. One audience member asked, "As heal-

> ### EXERCISE
>
>
>
> The next time you feel pressed down, ask yourself, "How is it that I am unenlightening myself?"

ers and spiritual leaders, we go through our own dark nights of the soul. How are we supposed to help someone through a crisis when we're in the middle of our own?"

He replied, "You realize that you are called for a reason. That reason is, as trained spiritual leaders, you can embrace the fact that you 'get to go through' things. You continue to stay present for the people we are helping."

I began to understand that by choosing a role as a spiritual leader, teacher, or healer, we have chosen to move beyond the level of amateur. But I also think that this is a good lesson for anyone on a serious spiritual path. You evolve into the understanding that **even when you are pressed down, you can use your awareness to learn and grow through the experience**.

Similarly, clinical professionals also practice being present like this for others. We are trained to create balance in our lives and to put our issues aside, temporarily, while in the presence of a patient or client. After all, they do not come to us to hear us vent, cry, or problem solve about ourselves. We must rise to the challenge to help them. We of course deal with our own issues but in an appropriate context. We commit to personal internal honesty. We consult another trusted healer, clinician, or a friend. If need be, we refer the client to another professional. We know how to separate our issue from another's and draw a healthy boundary.

EXERCISE

When you realize that ego got you, stop and ask, "How is it specifically that I am putting myself back in the illusion?"

No matter one's role, when you get on the path of spiritual evolution, you are propelled into greater dimensions of showing up in the world by virtue of your willingness to stay on the path. Inner freedom brings a change in your frame of reference. You don't get lost in problems. You come to grips with the fact that you cause your own suffering, and you come to know you can choose differently. You become **gifted** with finding newer and creative ways to respond to life all around you, in all types of relationships and settings. You remember that **even though you may be experiencing something upsetting, you are at the same time on your way out of it**. When you are living in this zone, you don't get tripped up in other people's stories or lapse into drama mode. You might recognize yourself on the edge of a flare up, but you have **become the observer**—emerging into pure consciousness. You realize that you can face your less than awakened parts. Now that you know about ego management and understand how to use forgiveness, those old ways of egoic thinking become like a snake skin you can shed.

ADDICTIONS AND REACTIONS

Some people would rather turn to addictive behaviors when they are stressed or pressed, but I encourage you to consciously decide to do something different. I invite you to think about how much alcohol you drink, how much food you eat, how much time you spend watching television, you name it—and cut back or eliminate alcohol, sugar, sodas, or television altogether. Returning to addictions are definitely not solutions I recommend when finding ways to manage stress, change, and upsets. Be **really honest** with yourself about this. You are highly creative and can find better options. One option is to remember your soul connecting activity that you enjoy, and do that instead.

HEALTHY COPING STRATEGIES

Try the following simple coping options when you feel pressed down:

— Drink warm tea or warm water with sliced lemon and freshly grated ginger and sit in a quiet space.

— Blend dark leafy greens with ginger, flax milk, and pineapple. Pour it into a fancy glass and top it off with an umbrella straw. Host a smoothie party!

— Turn on some music and dance all by yourself, or with a friend.

— Draw or paint whatever you like.

— Take a walk in nature. Get out and breathe fresh air.

— Lay back on your yoga mat doing nothing. Just surrender your body to the earth.

— Take a hot bath of Epson salts to soak out your stress.

— Close your eyes and envision relaxing in your favorite location.

— Pray or meditate.

— Record a prayer for someone else and send it through your phone or computer.

EXERCISE

Get out your markers, pens, and colored paper. Cut the paper into ten two-inch-wide by five-inch-long strips. On each, craft your own positive, affirming miracle-minded statements, prayers, and quotes. Use color and create your own designs. Place these around your house, office, in the car, in your purse. Give some away. Make this fun!

EXERCISE

Stop and say the following affirmations aloud.

- "I cope well with life's challenges and I handle stress with grace and ease."

- "I make choices from my highest, wisest self."

- "I am light and love, and I inspire others."

- "I choose healthy foods and drinks to nourish my whole being, even when I am stressed."

- "Thank you _____ (name your Source) for all that I am, for all that I have, and for this present challenge."

- "I know this challenge is only temporary."

- "I get out and explore nature regularly."

- "I am conscious of how facets of my soul are reflected in nature."

EXERCISE

Using the above as a reference, consider your own life "Bring it on" statement. Then state it aloud three times to affirm it.

— Do something nice for someone else—get out of your own head and story.

— Call someone you know and trust who will make you laugh and tell him or her, "I need a good laugh right now."

There are so many healthy ways to cope. Can you think of ten additional ways? Go ahead and write these in your journal.

I invite you to pause right now and sit with no distractions. Take three deep breaths. Now consider one thing that has been pressing on you recently. It can be anything, from a small detail or a disappointment to not getting a job that you wanted. Whatever it is, name the situation and consider what your typical response would be. Then think about what your best coping response could be.

Affirmations can help remind you to practice miracle mindedness on a daily basis. Let the positive energy from the affirmations be your elixir, your tonic, for healing and for releasing any stress.

State aloud, **"Aloha, life! Bring it on, I love challenges and change, and I want to blossom and evolve who I am. I love to grow and learn and to experience all parts of life, even the tough stuff. I can take it!"**

CHAPTER 16: BLOCKS

To reiterate, as you continue to spiritually deepen, you start to feel more alive, in tune, awake, and motivated. At the same time, at this stage in the process, people often tell me they feel "blocked" despite all of their hard work. It is okay to feel that way. No matter where you are on the spiritual path, you are sure to endure these moments where life hurls more challenges your way. In a way, this is life saying, "You can handle it all, and you can go deeper with spirit." As long as you are aware of this, you can open to it, manage it, and move through it.

Perhaps you are beginning to question if you came from an all-good and an all-loving Source. Maybe your friends or family are saying things about your new ways of being. They might label you different or treat you like you are "just going through a phase." They may even insinuate that you are "insane" or "wrong" for not believing in their type of spirituality or religion. They might be condescending, negative, or gossip about you. But now **you have built up your confidence**. You know those challenges are your teachers and that you "get to" experience these situations as lessons and gifts. Such trials can help you take **bigger and bolder steps** into living the life you dream of living. Remember: As you increase your consciousness, you also increase your responsibility. You realize that there are consequences to everything and you know that when you act from what is not true, you only cause yourself more pain.

By acting from a calm place, you can cultivate a new level of awareness in the presence of which ego finally becomes still. From this place, you can quickly discern if others are projecting their own fears onto you in the course of your interactions with them. Here is the gist: with each challenge life brings to you, might you see that those "blocks" aren't really blocks at all?

Reverend Michael Bernard Beckwith also tells us that this is the time to "play in the abyss of the deepest parts of yourself." You can dive into those cavernous waters and explore the vastness of your whole being! Remember that no one is judging you here. And please don't judge yourself. Right where you are on the path is perfect. Putting a baby toe in the water is good. Treading water is good; floating on your back is good; and learning to jump and then dive head first is all good too. Even if you make mistakes, it's all right. **Mistakes are a part of the plan. They keep you learning and leaning into life**. The idea is to **recognize any missteps, make course corrections, and get back on track**. Keep returning to your positive thoughts and your loving nature. With these practices you will balance the dream with the reality, the real, the unreal, the spiritual, the soulful, the ego, the mystery of it all.

Recognize that the "blocks" you might be experiencing at this point are actually perceived blocks. Even though you have allowed more light and truth in, the ego continues to keep its grip on you. It tries to slow you down, and put you in what it thinks is your rightful place. But this is not true. The ego is still trying to make you reactive, to feel dumb, different, out of place with society, guilty, angry, dramatic, silly, crazy, sinful, confused, and so forth. And, yes, this may be despite all of your good efforts. But **you can do this.** You can get past the deception because you know **YOU are the answer.** Remember to **ask ceaselessly, "Who am I?"** to get you back to your true self.

PHYSICAL BLOCKS

If you experience a set-back, you will need to examine your thoughts and feelings and check in with yourself often. Scan your body daily to note where you might literally be holding stress. Your "blockage" might come up as headache pain, back pain, sinus congestion, constipation, or dehydration.

Stop and check in with yourself physically right now. Just note any stress or pain or sensations. See if you have anything going on in your body. This can be either a positive or negative change. Try not to judge it. Just notice it and be with the sensations. Breathe into the experience as you do this. **Allow the energy to move through you.**

Every person is different but it is essential to note where stress typically manifests in your body. Once again, I am reminding you to change your thoughts so you can change how you feel. I am also reassuring you so you can release deeply embedded negative memes. Memes are deeply ingrained cultural norms and behaviors. One example is how the media portrays the ideal American woman—stick-thin, clad from head to toe in expensive clothing, high-powered career, schedule booked from 4:30 A.M. till midnight, relentless with her goals and walking over people to get what she wants. That kind of message is merely playing on ego needs.

Now that you know you are not those blocks and that they are erroneously in your way, can you **declare your oneness with the Source of all?** Can you not just consider but **know that you are an extension of the one loving Source** of all that is? You are soulful, source-full, and spirit-filled. You are the essence of God that is everywhere, and that energy is available at all times, and to everyone. You just need to take responsibility for re-acquainting yourself with it and claiming it. Absolutely know that the Source of life is in you, me, the flowers, the trees, the ocean, the chair you are sitting on, the book you are holding, the air, your car, the freeway—even in illusion and physical pain. You can also attain your life goals and be successful from this point of view.

At this point you have the knowledge, the skills, and the empowerment to start taking action on a daily basis to be your greatest self. The world needs you to function from your true loving nature. **The world needs you to stay aware, to stay open, to stay flexible, and to keep making those mental shifts.** The world needs more of this real you. You can enjoy this inner journey of deepening as you climb over life's "blocks," "rocks," and "boulders" with heroic efforts! You can weather the storm surges, the hurricanes, and the tsunamis of life! **You have the power within you** to define your own passions, to deflect the blocks, and to move from life "problems" to life "ventures." Maybe you can see all of life as one energetic source that keeps changing, and that **energy** is the true "task" to understand and manage.

I wrote the following affirmation. See if you can feel into this as a deep knowing for yourself:

> *"I am not my history or my past or my future. I am definitely*
> *not my ego. I am an extension of the divine, loving,*
> *mysterious, energetic Source of life. I can vibrate at higher*
> *energy frequencies and serve the world from this place."*

EXERCISE

Affirm aloud three times: "I am not those blocks. I am not those memes. No one and nothing gets in the way of my truth. I am a source of miracles, and I lovingly claim my light once and for all."

It is time to really begin to heed your soul calling. So, has your ʻuhane (soul) been whispering to you? Hopefully that inner voice is getting a little louder and clearer.

Are you willing to trust in the deeper waters of life? Can you allow yourself to fully feel your fears, all of them, then do what your soul is calling you to do anyway? You might not have the perfect plan yet and you might not have all the t's crossed and i's dotted, but you can keep working your "self improvement plan" you started in Chapter 7 and **trust** in the universe for guidance. All will be revealed. Trust. Surrender. Breathe. Let grace show you the way.

"I rule my mind,
which I alone must rule.
I thus set it free
to do the will of God."
—A Course in Miracles

"It is then that you will hear a voice within yourself. It was there all the time, but you never listened before. Faintly it will speak to you at first, but it will gradually grow louder and clearer the more you take heed of its message until one day it thunders inside you and you will have come home."

—*Kristin Zambuka*

CHAPTER 17: SHARING YOUR GIFTS

In this chapter I help you go deeper by encouraging you to see the importance of sharing your life gifts. **The universe needs you to be you and it is incomplete without you.** It is not pompous to know this. It is not at all pretentious to know that you can place yourself at the frontline of your life—**so you can actualize your potential.** This chapter ties in the work you did earlier with respect to clarifying and accepting your soul needs.

To gently remind you of the theme of this book, I do not want you to go to your deathbed wishing you had lived your life differently. You have a very unique purpose for being here, and only you can do the job of being you. **You came into this world to shine and to help others shine.** I want you to **make the globe glitter and radiate with your rareness!** Your soul is calling you to do this, and deep down inside you know the call is real. Once you connect with your Source and stay tuned to it, you will gain clarity on your calling. The answer is already within you, you just need to allow it to manifest.

IN SERVICE

The way we let ourselves shimmer is by using our divine gifts as kokua (as service or as help) to others. And that act is authentically powerful for everyone.

You do this by infusing your conscious loving energy into all you do. If you sincerely desire to share your soul calling with the world—as my friend Christine did with her love of nature and her call to demand justice as an arborist, and as my friend Tad did with his call to write and play music—then you can beam brilliantly in service also.

"Do you know what you are? You are a manuscript of a divine letter. You are a mirror reflecting a noble face. This universe is not outside of you. Look inside yourself: everything that you want, you are already that."

—*Rumi*

Defining, knowing, and living your gifts can give your life the deepest meaning. You may choose to share your gifts as a parent, in your work, as a volunteer, in your art, cooking, athleticism, healing, sportsmanship, teaching, writing, engineering, gardening, you name it! When you serve from this very deep way of walking in the world, you also emanate your conscious energy. And that energy becomes contagious. Others will be attracted to you for your radiating truth of being. The world will respond in kind to your intentions.

NATURE'S GIFTS

Just as Hawaii and all of Mother Earth gifts us with their beauty, it is your innate nature to gift others as well. One of the Attitudinal Healing principles that I learned from Dr. Jampolsky is "Giving is the same as receiving." I can tell you it feels great to be in this deeper flow with life; to know that when I give, I receive, and when I receive, I give.

Are you allowing yourself to appreciate the bountiful gifts of nature all around you and from within you? If not, I encourage you to get out more in nature to get inspired. Note the beauty all around you; this will help get you in touch with your innate abundance. Remember your calling is what you would do even if you did not get paid to do it. It is **what you feel you absolutely have to do, your reason, to be happy.**

EXERCISE

Reflect on the following statement: "Giving is the same as receiving."

When I started giving away my life coaching as gifts for silent auction benefit programs and as gifts to friends—people responded with generous offers to pay more. One lovely participant, who used to be a speaker and workshop leader, told me, "Honey, I would have given you fifty dollars just to draw my soul. I just loved that exercise." She helped me begin to better appreciate my true value and what was working. With her kindness, my energy intensified a bit more, and I was affirmed in my truth. As a result, my passion to teach and to give multiplied. My trusting muscle got a good workout too! This is how the world shows back up to us. When you are focused and working in alignment with spirit, the universe says, "Yes, love.

I've got your back, always." These were serious lessons in building my faith. I also learned to release from my timelines and trust in **divine timing**.

ART 'N SOUL

I always get excited about this next "art 'n soul" exercise. It is another unique creation of mine, and I often use it during my workshops in conjunction with my Aloha Ego process you were invited to try in chapter 10. Here, you are invited to play with your ego and your soul, as an artist, to help you gain more clarity on heeding your soul calling. This can be a simple yet compelling exercise. Consider the last time your ego showed up to you and what you felt like in your body. Now, name it if that feels right to you. For example, "scared ego" or "angry ego."

Follow the exercises (Parts I, II, and III on the next page).

Take a few deep breaths here. Note the difference in each of the facets of your personality. Feel the difference as you consider living life from your ego wants, needs, desires, etc., and then consider living life from your soul. Now turn to your soul drawing and ask,

1. "How do you want me to show up in the world?" Ask it, "What are you calling me to do?"

2. "How can I use my talents, gifts, and strengths to serve others?"

Then close your eyes and breathe. Listen to that inner voice. See if anything comes up for you. And if you get evidence on what it is, write it down, and write whatever pours out from you. If nothing comes up, let it be. Do try to stay tuned into any messages that may come up later.

As you become stronger spiritually and use your talents and skills to create more happiness and financial success in your life, you might at times experience confusion and conflict. After all, the really good things in life are immaterial, while we all want a life of prosperity and abundance—"success." Mind you there is nothing wrong with success, as long as you are inviting it and living it from a place of integrity and not getting lost in the material and un-loving aspects it often brings. Also, be open to how success forms, and when it arrives. For example, if you have a timeline set to complete a project but you come to realize that it may take twice as long to get the job done right, you will need to open up to discover the gifts in the waiting and in the learning and set a new timeline. Consider this as a flexible and open way of managing change and attaining your goals as opposed to a more rigid and controlling mind-set that does not appreciate the waiting and the long term benefits waiting often brings. This non-attachment to "the one and only way" to achieve something is an art form. Non-attachment is open and spacious. It can hold your intense longing, and it can hold possibility. Non-attachment understands that some things take time, that you have to meet the universe half way. You have to learn to see where your agenda fits in on the universe's schedule. It is also what I like to call a serious exercise in patience.

As you practice yielding, you also **stay committed and remain diligent** in your efforts to succeed. You can continue to do your part, your work setting goals and meeting those goals, and your inner spiritual work, by formulating those spiritually based life "business plans." You do your research on your goals. You take **responsibility.** You connect with inspiring people, and you take all the necessary steps you need to. You give it all you got, and then let go. Give it all up to the island universe to be worked on. Then allow it to come back with answers, a pot of gold, a new idea, a

EXERCISE

PART I

Get out some blank paper and your color pens, pencils, crayons, and markers. I invite you to first draw your ego. Feel into it. Put a face to it in your mind's eye or just note the visual of it as you consider this exercise. It could be abstract. It could be anything. Just use your imagination. Turn the ego drawing face down. Proceed to Part II.

EXERCISE

PART II

On a separate sheet of paper, draw your soul. Breathe into it. What does it feel like? What comes up in your mind's eye?

EXERCISE

PART III

Now turn the ego drawing over, and put the ego and soul drawings next to each other. Go back to page 204 and read where you left off.

"The best way to find your self is to lose yourself in the service of others."
—*Mahatma Gandhi*

breakthrough, an alternative, a treasure chest, a home. Remain open to things happening sooner or later. Stay open to new ideas that may take you in a bit of a different direction. All the while, stay true to the innermost desires of your heart: your values, your relationships, your purpose. Remember, being rigid is not what you are going after. Bear in mind that you also want to watch your inner language and how you are speaking with yourself.

Hilina'I (believe) in the higher power of the one divine mind. Remember to have fun with all this! Remain balanced as you are being nudged to use your wise-heart with any changes you are considering. The combination of intelligence and heart-centeredness is a perfect blend and not at all mutually exclusive.

You soul might be calling you to contemplate changes such as starting a new career, buying a business, selling a business, selling everything, or get-

ting a new job, staying in your job, having a baby or adopting a baby, travelling around the world, getting married or getting a divorce, taking social action, or moving to a new location. You name it. No matter your change, you can create intelligent, heart-centered plans, and put yourself on a path of glorious new beginnings—continuing to make your heart sing.

Stay inspired and motivated. As you move forward and as you appreciate each moment wherever you are, let the sun (la) and the moon (mahina) be your guides. **Appreciate the rain and then look for rainbows.** Each day you have an opportunity to re-birth (hanauhou). Each day you can be better than you were yesterday. Keep igniting that inner ruckus. Let your courage be contagious. Keep trying

EXERCISE

Now you get to synthesize what you have learned so far and how you might start to share your gifts. Stop now and breathe. Take three deep breaths. Ask yourself, "What does my indwelling Source need me to do with all of the life questions I have been answering and the exercises I've been completing throughout this book?" "What is my next step, if there is a next step?" Take a few moments to sit in silence here. Allow spirit to shower you with the answers that you are seeking.

new things, but also give yourself permission to be, and let your soul dance and sing no matter what!

By completing the above exercise, you will be prepared to make your final legacy statement and your life purpose statement in the next few chapters.

"Our deepest fear is not that we are inadequate. Our deepest fear is that we are powerful beyond measure. It is our light, not our darkness that most frightens us. We ask ourselves, who am I to be brilliant, gorgeous, talented, and fabulous? Actually, who are you not to be? You are a child of God. Your playing small does not serve the world. There is nothing enlightened about shrinking so that other people

won't feel insecure around you. We are all meant to shine, as children do. We were born to make manifest the glory of God within us. It's not just in some of us; it's in everyone. And as we let our own light shine, we unconsciously give other people permission to do the same. As we are liberated from our own fear, our presence automatically liberates others."
—*Marianne Williamson*

"Are you searching for your soul? Then come out of your own prison. Leave the stream and join the river that flows into the ocean. When you do things from your soul, you feel a river moving in you, a joy. You have no need to travel anywhere. Journey within yourself. Enter a mind of rubies and bathe in the splendor of your own light."

—*Rumi*

Act III: Riding the Wave to the Shore
CHAPTER 18: TRUTH

This is a good time to pause and recap the main ideas in the previous Acts. In Act I you were invited to prepare to dive into your spiritual essence. You were given quite a few life prescriptions for preparing, waking up, clarifying, and cleaning. Act II invited you to dive in by accepting, practicing, and deepening with spirit. You were able to clean up the past so you could heal and make room to move forward. In Act III you now have an opportunity to fully integrate all of your hard work. The remaining chapters prescribe embracing, intuiting, and celebrating exercises. This is your chance to dive in to catch the wave and ride it all the way in to the shore, enjoying and surrendering to the flow of life.

PELE

In chapter 17 you were guided to go deeper by considering how you could share your spiritual gifts with the world. In this chapter you are invited to take that a step further to embrace those gifts with the energy of **Pele** (the Hawaiian Fire Goddess): she can help you get in touch **your innermost red, hot, fiery truth** for living your soul calling and igniting your passion for living your true purpose for being in the world. These next few chapters will help you solidify your understanding of your life purpose.

In Hawaii, the spirit of Pele is very much alive. Pele is closely linked with spiritual traditions of native Hawaii. She is also known as the divine spark of creation, an aspect of the divine mother, found in traditions around the world. I once heard that Pele is like the housekeeper of our planet. Mount Kilauea is a large active volcano on the Big Island of Hawaii where Pele lives. According to legend, when Pele is moved to do so, she will ignite a fabulous

"Humankind has not woven the web of life. We are but one thread within it. Whatever we do to the web, we do to ourselves. All things are bound together. All things connect."
—*Chief Seattle*

fire show that shoots molten hot lava up into the sky and rolling down into the sea, forming new land.

Are you ready to **claim new landscapes of you**? Pele wants to inspire you to do just that. Pele is described as having a wide range of emotions. She gets angry and jealous, and she is soft and kind. She even practices forgiveness. I believe Pele forgives those who throw trash on her island home, and those who attempt to destroy her new landscapes. The activity of Pele reminds me of our human nature and that we are all capable of igniting that fire within and renewing ourselves to live deeper and more meaningful lives. Much as the 'aina (land) itself continues to be reborn, so do you. You can consciously make this choice for yourself. Are you willing to get in touch with your inner Pele?

DIVINE FEMININE

Feel, hear, and heed the call of your Goddess nature, by whatever name you have for it. Men can claim their divine feminine as well. The time has come to step further into the feminine. I feel strongly that we are all responsible for stoking the psychic flame of our inner Pele so we can create new ways of functioning in the world, to balance the masculine with the feminine. I like to think we are moving from masculine, hyper-competitive, money hungry, win-at-all-costs attitudes to co-creating a more loving, peaceful, and stable planet.

Your divinity is waiting for you. Your legacy is waiting for you. Your life purpose is waiting for you. It is likely that your inner Pele has been napping and you may have lost touch with that inner flame. But now you can wake up and re-ignite it. We all know that life is short, and we can no longer afford to move on auto-pilot. We can no longer wait; the keiki (children) of the world need our efforts now.

Fill in the blank: I am willing to commit to _____ in order to connect further with my highest self.

When your inner Pele is ready, aware, and curious enough, those dormant forces come alive and there is no holding back. You will take bigger and bolder steps as Pele dances wildly for you. She shakes you and the ground that you walk on. She rattles your insides to stimulate you to take **FEARLESS, FORWARD STEPS.** You begin to radiate higher energy frequencies.

"'When a great storm comes,'
they told her mother, 'your
ancestors will bring the spirit
of your child.' One night,
'when the earth shook,
lightning split the sky, and
thunder rolled down the
green valleys,' Pele arrived."
—*Varez and Kanahele, from the
book* Pele Fire Goddess

You will notice more and more miracle moments, and in this space life doesn't feel as difficult as it once did.

Take three deep breaths. See if you can feel the passions of Pele desiring to come forth. Invoke Pele as the mystical feminine whose time has come. She represents the deep truth of you that has been bubbling at the core, only temporarily suppressed by our culture, ego, and society's standards. She is prepared, having done her job of tending to the embers, your pain, your stories which have held you back, your confusion, anxiety, dramas, and fears you have been clinging to. Yet she is never wavering, never losing her spark. She is ready to rise from within you and get you back on course.

ENERGY CENTERS WITH YOGA

The energy centers in your body are also known as "Chakras." This is a Sanskrit word describing the spinning wheels of energy at seven different points along the body. As you proceed envision the colored wheels spinning with energy down the mid line of your body.

Go ahead and sit up taller in your chair. Raise your arms to the side and then over your head with palms facing each other. Feel yourself rising up. Now open your heart Chakra (sometimes called the Thymus Chakra; it governs the emotions). With eyes closed see it as a green ball of light. Now open your heart Chakra by opening your arms wide to form a "V" and slowly tilt your head back keeping your eyes closed. Note your heart center opening

EXERCISE

Contemplate the questions below, then journal on the ones that resonate most with you. Remember to activate your audaciousness!

1. How am I going to make a difference in my life and in the world?
2. How might I serve children or future generations?
3. How can I practice peace, daily?
4. How can I love my neighbors?
5. How might I use my creativity and artistic expression?
6. Will I write my own memoir to let others know that they are not alone on their journey?
7. Will I commit to mindfulness practices and hold a positive attitude?
8. Will I commit to shifting from my ego to my soul, daily?
9. Where might I volunteer?
10. Could I begin a contemplative yoga practice?
11. Will I donate time, money, skills, and my abilities to organizations that resonate with my values?
12. Will I change my career to pursue what I truly love to do?
13. Can I commit to stop selling my soul—to stop doing the things I know I do not truly want to be doing and allow something greater to emerge?
14. How might I help animals, nature, and the environment?

"Because of her great power, people tend to think that Pele is a destroyer. But she isn't. She will reclaim land that has been desecrated by humankind, but she always provides us with an opportunity to keep the

balance. If we do not, then by all means Pele will reclaim that land. But she is not destroying; she is reclaiming and restoring."
—*Sondra Ray from the book* Pele's Wish

as you stretch. Note that you are physically opening. Breathe in and feel the inflow and outflow of your breath. Feel the expansion of your life unfurling into its destiny. Now, try this exercise again by closing your eyes and feeling Goddess Pele's warm energy moving through your body. Imagine connecting with Pele in your energy centers by visualing each center as a spinning wheel of light from your toes to your legs, then up to your root Chakra (lower pelvis; color: red; it governs power, money, and sex) then up to the naval (pancreas, spleen; color: orange; it is the inner child) then up through your solar plexus (adrenal glands; color: yellow; it governs survival issues), back to the heart (green), and throat (thyroid; color: cobalt blue; it is the seat of truth, creativity), then up to your third eye between the eyebrows (pituitary; color: light blue or teal; from it emanate the psychic abilities), and then up and out through your crown Chakra (top of the head; color: purple; it is the center of spiritual enlightenment). Breathe. Affirm how beautiful, brilliant, and powerful your body temple is.

EXERCISE

Try the gentle yoga practice I just described, noting your energy centers. Feel slowly into your body and listen to what it is saying to you. Back off if anything is uncomfortable or if you feel any pain.

Immerse yourself in the present moment of abundant love as you feel the energy emanating within. Take three deep breaths and return to a relaxed and seated position and then gently back into the room. Note your sensations and write down any ideas that may arise. Note where your energy centers may feel enlivened, or maybe a bit off, or any sensation you may have experienced. Be with the experience for a few moments and try it again if you need to. You can practice this exercise at anytime, and you can ask a friend to do it with you.

Pele wants you to call forth her energy for life and to enjoy doing it. As you connect with her she will remind you of your strength, courage, power, passions, brilliance, and beauty. Hold these dynamic thoughts of this Pele energy as you move into the next chapter.

Affirm: **"I feel the hotness of Pele burning deep in my soul. I am awake, alive, and on fire with life!"**

CHAPTER 19: FULL CIRCLE

This chapter will bring you full circle to integrate the death-dying and life-living and soul-purpose exercises you have been working on. As promised, you will be guided to create your final legacy statement and your final life purpose statement. You may have made a few drafts of these by now, which is just perfect. Consciously choosing to embrace death as a part of life, and living a focused, inspired, and self-actualized life, is not something many people get around to. This is something to take in deep within the center of your being; acknowledge it and honor it.

One health research study by Andrew Steptoe, Director of the University College London Institute of Epidemology and Health Care, shows that people with life purpose live longer. He says this is "because they have a level of autonomy and sense of control in their own life." Just as you eat healthy foods and exercise to take care of your body, seeking a meaningful life of purpose nourishes the spirit—and as contemporary research shows, improves your physical and emotional health as well. Let us all choose to live longer and with greater freedom and heightened self direction so we can ride out every wave of change with peace, joy, resilience, zest, faith, and authentic power. It is time to finally claim it in your heart, in your mind, and in your soul—for the greater good of all.

Working with hundreds of complicated medical cases has provided opportunities for me to witness how short and precious life really is. One of the most rewarding things I have ever done is to have helped chronically ill patients—ranging in age from 19 to 99—name their legacy, and help them to live it more fully with the time they had left. I have had some challenging conversations as I help the families talk about their fears of their loved ones dying and their anticipated grief. When I ask the question about the patient's legacy, they are at first astounded and then appreciative, telling me that no one has ever asked them those questions before. No matter where they were with their disease process, I have had very few patients tell me they can't talk about the inevitable. With the legacy framework I provide, I help them make critical care choices, and they often thank me. I love this part of my work because I make heartfelt and powerful connections with people who seem to walk away with greater peace. Several patients have said similarly, "That legacy thing is better than any prescription any doctor ever gave me." Well, there is an idea—what if doctors actually did recommend that people get in touch with their life purpose? What if other institutions encouraged this or offered courses in this as well—middle schools, high schools, colleges, churches, spiritual centers?

By now you know that the goal of this book has been to get you to embrace your life from a deeply powerful place, so that you do not wait until you are sick or dying to think about how you want to be remembered or what's been missing from your life. If there was only one prescription, formula, or recipe I had to give anyone it would be: **BEGIN TO KNOW AND LIVE YOUR LEGACY NOW.** I firmly believe that the world would be a much healthier place if there were more people who were focused on living their life purpose.

In chapters 6 and 7, the clarifying section of the book, I asked you to begin thinking about your legacy and your life purpose and to draft your epitaph. I've also invited you to consider your strengths, weaknesses, values, and to assess various domains of your life. You have cleaned up the past, you have tamed your ego, and embraced your spirituality. You are groomed to fully embrace those foundational concepts and integrate the prescriptive exercise that I will now lay out for you. You are now being asked to **fiercely focus for one week** as you claim your legacy and your life purpose. You might need less time, depending on how far you have taken the exercises thus far. Whatever amount of time you need, I urge you to **devote yourself** to the time you set aside.

FULL CIRCLE EXERCISES—FOCUS AND INTEGRATION

At the beginning of your week, usually on a **Monday**, block an hour in the morning and evening when you have sufficient alone time. If you are a parent of small children you may want to use their nap time for your writing and reflection. If you are limited on your time, please consider how you might re-priortize for one week. Your task during this time is to ask yourself the following questions, "Why do I get up in the morning?" "Who am I?" "Why am I here?" "What is my soul calling?" Your goal is to stay focused on these questions and possible answers that may arise within you. Integrate all of the lessons in your process. Ignore any thoughts such as, "My family thinks I...," "My partner thinks I...," "My wife thinks I...," or "My husband thinks I...." Let this exercise be just for you. If you need to, go back and review your initial thoughts on your legacy in your journal. Read the drafts you prepared.

> ## EXERCISE
>
>
>
> For one week, block out some time on your calendar and complete the following daily assignments.

You can take a walk as you reflect or view nature through a window. The important thing is to commit to doing it. Remember to connect with your breathing. Keep your work private. Consider this as a sacred exercise for yourself. After you reflect, journal your reflections on the question.

On **Tuesday**, in the same block of time, consider your strengths and your innate talents. Think about your skills and what you love to do, the activities that bring you the most joy. Write them on one page of your journal. List everything that comes up. The list needs to come from your heart and not be influenced by what others might think. For example, I would list, "teaching, practicing yoga, spirituality, Hawaiiana, writing, being with friends, meditating with the sunrise, walking on the beach, hiking, reading, and dancing."

Then circle the top three that bring you the most joy. Within these three, circle the one that gets you totally blissed out. It is likely it will be the same "go to" activity that you tried in chapter 13, but not necessarily.

On **Wednesday**, in the same time block you previously allotted, consider your values. Ask yourself, "What do I truly value in life?" Now list these. Then circle your very top choice. If you already did this earlier, you're done, unless you feel called to change it now.

On **Thursday,** begin by reflecting on the following question, "How do I want people to remember me after I die?" (Again, try to use the same time block you have been using and do this going forward if you can. This routine can help you stay on course.) Now, write your epitaph by combining your top strength/talent with your value that you just listed. Ask yourself, "If I were to die tomorrow, what would my tombstone say?"

Here is my example of a legacy statement that I would want someone to read at my Celebration of Life Memorial Service before my ashes are to be spread across the deep, blue heavenly seas at Lanikai beach:

> *"She loved to use her writing, yoga, social work, and*
> *creativity to inspire people to live with more peace,*
> *playfulness, purpose, and prosperity. She was a teacher,*
> *an example, and a lover of Hawaii. She taught us to live*
> *our legacies. Her soul is dancing the hula somewhere off in*
> *the great mystery, and her love will be with us forever."*

On **Friday,** spin your epitaph into your life purpose statement. You will be turning your epitaph statement into a positive life affirming statement you can develop even further.

Here is my life purpose statement that I keep in a frame on my home office desk:

> *"As a child of the divine, my purpose and passion in life is to be*
> *and teach peace. I lovingly use my creativity to inspire others*
> *to live their highest selves. I claim my skills and talents as*
> *an author, teacher, yogi, social worker, and lover of Hawaii.*
> *I inspire others to live their legacies. My soul dances the*
> *hula and forever remains unlimited universal potential."*

Take delight with this, and be resolute. Take the time to make this your "make the globe glisten and gleam by your presence" statement.

On **Saturday**, allow some extra time to get creative. Use your imagination to make your life purpose statement stand out. You may want to color it or paint it. I highly encourage you to frame it. **Let your creative genius emerge with this!** Try to keep the statement to about six sentences or fewer. I suggest keeping this sacred object either on your nightstand, your desk, or your altar (see examples for setting up an altar in the later chapter on Full Presence Awareness). Keep it where you'll see it upon waking and before retiring each day. You can also incorporate your life purpose statement in a celebration that you will be asked to hold in the last chapter. Use your imagination—you could make bookmarks of it and place it in your books, place them in your purse or checkbook, or on the dashboard of your car. Heck, you might want to put them in even more interesting and fun places where you can find them later, like in the cookie jar, in a vase, in a shoe, or in between dishes. Infuse this life energy anywhere and everywhere!

On **Sunday**, set aside a few hours for reflection on your life purpose statement. Consider the following:

1.   Ask yourself, "Am I practicing living what I plan to leave?"

2.   Then ask, "How will I start practicing living my life purpose today if I haven't already?"

3.   If you need to, buy a project management notebook to keep yourself organized as you reach goal after goal and as you further plan and unfold your life mission. Keep this sacred book as your life business plan.

4.   Continue to dedicate time on a daily basis to allow for journaling and reflection.

If you are ever in doubt about your plans, take a walk, meditate, pray, or write. The point is to get started and waste no more time. Having just said that, it is also essential to allow yourself plenty of time to just "be." You don't want to get caught up in the "doing." Honor yourself, get plenty of rest, and reflect. Remember to balance everything as best as you can and not beat yourself up when you make mistakes. This is all a part of living your soul centeredness, learning, growing, evolving.

One of the most profound books I have ever read on life purpose is *Man's Search for Meaning* by Viktor Frankl. In 1942, Frankl, a prominent Jewish psychiatrist and neurologist in Vienna, was arrested and transported to a Nazi concentration camp, separated from his family. He was there for three years and he clung to the idea that his wife might still be alive. He knew he had to find meaning in the idea that even though things were grim, there was still a *possibility* she could be alive. As he saw in the camps, those who found meaning even in the most horrific circumstances were far more resilient in the face of suffering than those who did not. Frankl tells how he helped two suicidal inmates. Like others in the camp, they were depressed and hopeless. They thought there was nothing left to live for. Frankl says "it was a question of getting them to realize that life was still expecting something from them; that something in the future was expected of them." For one of the men, it was his young child. And for the other man, a scientist, it was a series of books he needed to complete. He says it is the "why" for existence that matters, and therefore one will be able to bear almost any "how." Frankl helps us to understand the emphasis on meaning, the value of suffering, and responsibility to something greater than the self.

Furthermore, according to the Center for Disease Control, about four out of ten Americans have not discovered a satisfying life purpose. Research has shown that having a purpose and a sense of meaning in life increases overall well-being and satisfaction, improves mental and physical health, enhances resiliency and self-esteem, and decreases the chances of depression.

So I passionately implore you, if you have any doubts about finding and living your pupose at this point, waste no more time. Breathe. Read and re-read where you need to. Find and make the time to answer the tough questions and dive into the exercises. The last chapters will give you even more resources to help you manifest your life purpose.

"Everything can be taken from man but one thing, the last of the human freedoms—to choose one's attitude in any given set of circumstances, to choose one's own way."
—*Viktor Frankl*

RX: EMBRACING

CHAPTER 20: SOUL FOOD PRESCRIPTIONS

Congratulations on completing your life legacy and life purpose statements! You have delved deep into some serious life changing work most people never get around to. It is my hope that you feel nourished from deep within your cells and that you are ignited to live every day from your core.

Now that you are clear on it, to help you practice living your life purpose, I've created a list of prayerful affirmations to help you stay in alignment with your soul calling. These are your soul food prescriptions. I hope you will be able to see that the prescriptive reminders are just as important to you as your daily nutrition or basic hygiene.

Consider printing your favorite soul food prescriptions from the list below and put them up by your medicine cabinet or on your refrigerator. You can refer to them as you eat, brush your teeth, put on deodorant, or brush your hair.

- Thank you spirit (Source, God, Holy Spirit, you name it) for this day.

- I consciously step into this day aligned with my highest self.

- I make wise choices throughout the day from the divine mind.

- I am an instrument of peace and love.

- I am abundant in every way.

- I observe the observer in myself.

- I keep ego in check by saying "Aloha, ego."

- I accept non-duality. We are all connected.

- My choices are critical to the life I dream of living.

- My choices are critical to others, plants, animals, and to the planet.

- I shift my mind and I create miracles often.

- I choose the miracle.

- I express my unique self in everything that I do.

- I note how my body feels and the thoughts that I am thinking.

- I live boldly. I wake up and get out of the tribe, and I row my own boat.

- I offer my talents and skills to others who need it.

- I give generously, and wisely, of my time, talent, and money.

- I serve without expectation and with genuine love.

- I stop to take conscious breaths throughout the day.

- I create something new and different.

- I forgive myself and others frequently.

- I am ready, open and available to new ideas and opportunities.

- I eat healthy, whole, and alive foods that nourish my body temple.

- I move my body and exercise regularly.

- I cut out or seriously limit alcohol.

- I am a teacher of and a learner with people.

- I am already free.

- I am whole and complete.

- I just need some fine tuning.

- I have choices in how I respond to others.

- I know what I want.

- I know how to research things.

- I am prepared and prepped for how I really want to be living.

- I can choose peace at any moment.

- I have a burning "Madam Pele" desire for life!

- I take active steps toward my goals.

- I educate myself. I do my homework. I ask. I explore.

- I build my confidence.

- I know that we are always either coming from a place of fear or of love.

- I feel the fear then I do what I need to do.

- I try new things and if something doesn't work, I have fun trying again.

- I get enough sleep and take glorious naps.

- I honor and respect all living creatures.

- I keep up a positive attitude.

- I note the goodness in others.

- I send silent blessings to others.

- I give myself ample alone time.

- I am resilient and move through challenges as I am aligned with spirit.

- I see moments of opportunity then I seize them.

- I see goodness, and God-ness all around me.

- I honor the Earth.

- I embrace challenges.

- I give thanks, many times, every day.

- I stop to behold nature.

- I find myself in nature.

- I claim my brilliance, beauty, and light.

- I detach from outcomes and time lines. I know there is divine timing.

- My life is in divine order, and I accept more good that is already on the way.

- I surrender.

- I trust.

- I embrace sacred moments and my divinity.

EXERCISE

Consider adding any additional "prescriptions" that motivate you. Write them in your journal, post them where you will be reminded of them daily, create a collage, or find your own creative ways to express them.

Chapters 20 and 21 are designed to help you further embrace your life purpose and spiritual essence on a daily basis. Please do not skip these last chapters. I have added them as bonus chapters, and I promise they will help you manifest the life you have designed, as long as you implement the practices.

CHAPTER 21: PROSPERITY CONSCIOUSNESS

Hawaii has filled me with unique experiences that reshaped my way of being in life. When I breathe in the scent of plumeria flowers, I literally soften and feel a sense of completeness. My heart skips a beat when I see waterfalls as I drive along the Pali Highway. After a good rainfall dozens of the waterfalls pour down the velvety and emerald green Ko'olau Mountains on the windward side of Oahu. My soul becomes rejuvenated when I take deep jungle hikes like the adventurous "Commando" hike near Hana, Maui. I feel at one with nature as I swim with dolphins near Makena, also on Maui. I feel that I'm in the flow of life when I paddle a kayak from Kailua Beach Park out to the Mokulua Islands in Lanikai. These experiences are rich. They make me feel lavish, naturally wealthy, unlimited, and overflowing with appreciation.

NATURAL ABUNDANCE

Just as the land in Hawaii is **prosperous, verdant, and lush**, so are you! As the universe is full of **infinite possibility**, so are you! We are all waves of energy and capable of embodying and expressing the highest frequencies of love. Would you like to know this on your deepest cellular level? If you desire an abundant life, it's important that you think and feel abundantly on a regular basis. This way of being takes your spirituality and life purpose to new dimensions. To **nurture your prosperity consciousness,** you will need to embrace positive thinking and abundant doing on a day-to-day and moment-by-moment basis. Every chapter has encouraged this so far. Now, you can fully learn to embody the practice of affluence.

The authors Esther Hicks and the late Jerry Hicks are two important teachers who inspire others to create a prosperity consciousness. Their writings have helped me to understand the value of living from within the vortex of spirit energy. They helped me break the chains of the poverty consciousness, or slave consciousness, I was once mired in. By undoing those old thought patterns I affirmed my worth and found wealth from within as well as all around me. I've also come to know that I am worthy of living my life purpose. In Hawaii, the natural landscape is readily available, generous, and beautiful, and for every trip back home I feel more connected and more peaceful. Practicing prosperity consciousness has allowed me to appreciate more, get out of my head, and open to a naturally abundant life from my heart and soul. When I did this my actual finances changed as well.

> ## EXERCISE
>
>
>
> In your journal list at least ten ways you note riches in nature and in the stars.

Wherever you may be at this time, pause and note how nature inspires you toward your own sense of abundance.

Next are some resources to further develop your sense of worthiness for abundance in all its forms. With practice they can become so ingrained in you that prosperity consciousness becomes a **natural** part of your way of living. It is important to build this into your way of thinking and behaving, so you are well equipped when those murky flash floods of life appear without warning.

Prosperity consciousness is about **living deliberately in all domains** of your life and telling the highest part of yourself the story you want to experience in life. This involves acknowledging every negative thought and turning it around to a positive thought as quickly as possible so it becomes habit.

VISUALIZATION

Visualization is also a key tool in creating a prosperous mindset. Take time to visualize what you want to experience every day. For example, if you want to take a trip around the world, close your eyes and experience what it feels like to adventure in far away cities. Imagine yourself there. Try to be in the experience as much as possible as you visualize. Note your senses as you explore in your mind's eye.

By **staying aligned** with your Source and working your plans, you will see gradual shifts in your life. Remember to stay open to new possibilities and to divine timing. The universe has a remarkable way of taking care of you when you are in tune with it.

As I've stayed true to these practices, many resources revealed themselves to me. I have gone from being jobless and broke to tripling my income in one year. I didn't sit by waiting for things to happen though. I was attending to my spiritual practices and volunteering at organizations in alignment with my values. I was researching, applying for jobs, and networking. I was aware of my thought habits, stayed actively focused, and did not allow myself to get sidetracked as I had in the past.

You must **stay tuned in, concentrated, and self-disciplined in addition to remaining non-attached** to get the results you intend to manifest. You can't expect everything to happen right when you want it to. Remember to **practice patience and faith**. Your perception should be I "get to" practice diligence.

MASTERING YOUR MIND

Prosperity consciousness is about a shift in energy which all starts in your mind. The very cells in your body have to **desire** the results you intend. And since your mind is connected to everything, you must **nurture** it. You have to master your mind, not have it master you. Now you know you have to retrain it from the conditions society has set upon it. When you start thinking, feeling, and acting from a place of positive energy, all things will line up for you. **You must shift internally before the outer change starts to take place**.

New possibilities reveal themselves when you are ready to open to them, such as the right person, book, idea, relationship, or job. But you must be awake enough and also be sustaining your own prosperity consciousness to notice it. Affirm the good. Affirm the right outcome. Affirm the truth. Let any negative, demeaning, or condescending remarks from others float on by you. You need not waste any time entertaining that kind of energy. **Stay in your zone of higher consciousness.**

EXERCISE

Affirm "I want to feel good." "I want to thrive in all areas of my life." "I can do (blank)." Fill in that blank.

Consider where you are on the spectrum between having a prosperity consciousness to prosperity unconsciousness. Write about this in your journal and note where you can make some shifts to make your awareness more robust.

If you think you are poor, you will be poor. If you are in a negative space, you have pinched yourself off from who you are supposed to be. Being negative is to be out of touch with your Source and your internal guidance system. Create those generous thoughts for others as well. Even if your bank account is temporarily poor, you are not. You can still give generous silent blessings and prayers from your **inner unlimited trust fund. Remember you are an heir or an heiress to an unlimited fortune—heaven is on Earth right here and now.** This is God, Spirit, Source energy moving in, through, and as you.

Be mindful of every thought and word and leave no room for doubts that you are manifesting the life you dream of living.

Choose thoughts that are **flexible**, not fixed, not soft, not hard. Think with **humility**, not smugness. Inject energetic thoughts into your everyday thinking. Wake up every day saying, **"Thank you, thank you, thank you,** spirit, for this day."** Feel appreciation for what you do have and state your appreciation for your life as it is and for all that is evolving. Know that you and your life are actively evolving.

Regularly visualize what you want to create. You will feel gradual shifts taking place as you visualize. You were born a being of unlimited value in an unlimited universe. Your birthright as a child of the divine demonstrates your worthiness—but you have to claim it.

EXERCISE

Affirm "I want to feel good. Nothing is more important than feeling good."

FINANCIAL PROSPERITY

The teachings of Eric Butterworth, set forth in a book titled, *Spiritual Economics*, help us understand that **we are living magnets for money, the energy of money that is**. He tells us that money is energy. I learned to see money as an extension of me and I must keep my identity with money as a symbol of limitless God substance (or energy).

Living your spiritual mission will act like a lure, and the velocity of the world arranges itself to support your creation. Stay in alignment with spirit, claim prosperity and wholeness in every area of your life. Dedicate your life purpose and spiritual mission to the healing of the world—then see what happens!

You draw to yourself the things, people, and the circumstances, including your financial condition, that are in accord with your thoughts. **Your fortune, good or bad, begins with you**.

Pause for a moment and consider what your reaction was to the recent economic recession. Did you react from faith or fear?

As you now know **wealth is in your ideas and your thinking**. Begin to see that **money is spirit in action**. Practice having discipline of mind to help you feel prosperous all of the time.

Money is a good thing, despite what we may have been told. I remember my mom saying, "Money doesn't grow on trees!" Then there was the tension and stress and upset feelings behind that statement that made me feel horrible at that time. What early childhood teachings about money do you still cling to? Send those old negative money thoughts far out to sea with hurricane force winds. Start to see money as a currency of creative love and divine activity.

Don't say, "I only have $_____." If you want more money, you cannot have thoughts of lack or "poor me" attitudes. Re-shape your attitudes toward yourself and make changes in how you spend or save money. Enjoy paying your bills! Develop an attitude of **gratitude** for being able to pay the bills even if you can only afford to pay a small amount. Just know you are working your way toward being able to pay more on those bills and then create a solid plan to do that.

EXERCISE

As you did in the beginning, stop and write out ten things you are grateful for in your life right now. Really feel how your body is responding to your state of appreciation. Note that the things you are appreciating might be different than the ones you initially chose.

EXERCISE

Go to your journal or your project management notebook and outline your budget and bill paying process if you do not currently have a system. Get yourself organized and commit to your overall wealth management program. This can be a highly spiritual endeavor.

"Here's the gift of gratitude. In order to feel it, your ego has to take a backseat. What shows up in its place is greater compassion and understanding. Instead of being frustrated you choose appreciation. And the more grateful you become, the more you have to be grateful for."

—Oprah

I keep a motivational card from the International Center for Attitudinal Healing as the divider between my checks. It reminds me to write something positive on the "for" section of the check. It reminds me to state my appreciation out loud for being able to pay the bills. Affirm: "I respect and appreciate my bills. They provide me with the essentials of life. I demonstrate responsibility and pay my bills on time."

Having lived at one time with immense anxiety about paying bills, this was a huge step for me. And I've made enormous leaps with my overall understanding and care for money as an energetic force for good. Remember—money is equal to spiritual principle and that is real capital! **Your character, your integrity, and your service are wealth!** If you need to, create a plan with your finances and keep working it.

Make it a habit to bless your money and your bills. What can you say to your money? How might you befriend your bill paying process?

Affirm the following out loud.

- I am worthy of good in my life.

- I enjoy the flow of good in all areas of my life.

- Life is abundant.

- There is enough abundance for everyone.

- I think good thoughts about money.

- I embody the energies of abundance.

- I lovingly take responsibility for my bills and debts.

- With joy I activate a wise investment plan.

- I joyfully express my inner worth.

- The universe supports me as I live my spiritual mission.

- I enjoy saving money and feeling how awesome it feels.

- I invest in my whole being.

- I give generously of my time, talent, and money.

- I am an heiress/heir to an unlimited trust fund of wisdom, creativity, compassion, divine ideas, joy, and love.

- I embrace prosperity consciousness for the greater good of all.

"When you really know yourself as a spiritual being, you experience the fulfilling of the law, which 'rushes, streams, and pours into you' in terms of substance and supply and all that is required for success."
—*Eric Butterworth*

CHAPTER 22: STABILIZED PRESENCE

Staying in touch with your Pele energy, prosperity consciousness, and living your legacy is not always easy. Living a spiritual life requires you to maintain a stabilized presence and to evolve it. You have been building a solid foundation for this way of living and you are responsible for maintaining it.

In this chapter I encourage you to **honor your body temple** by increasing your time in meditation, and I will teach you about positive practical prayer so you **feel intuitively connected with your Source as a sixth sense**. Such prayer can lay the foundation for the **authentically powerful and spiritually grounded loving empire of you**.

With intuition you learn to ask, "What would God, Jesus, Akua, Buddha, Mary, Pele, or _____ have me do with this situation?" (Fill in that blank). Remember, **you are an extension of Source,** by whatever name you have been giving it.

I wish someone had taught me this "trick" of relating to my intuition and spirituality like this in my childhood! For me, this is how to really be in the world. But, like many, I was not taught to know my true self as a child and was given plenty of mixed messages that seriously confused me. In fact, as were many others, I was taught to ignore the wise part of me. As a child in the South, children are often treated as "seen but not heard." I would ask lots of questions and not get a lot of answers. As a Southern female, I was taught to place emphasis on how to "look pretty." So when my curious mind wanted answers, I was ignored. As you now know from a few stories I have shared with you, there was a lot of drama, poverty, depression, grief, lack of education, and alcoholism around me as I grew up. I was taught to deny the higher parts of myself from well intended people who happened to be very lost themselves.

"I have come to drag you out of yourself and take you into my heart. I have come to bring out the beauty you never knew you had and lift you like a prayer to the sky."
—*Rumi*

Yet we all must move on from such long-past experiences once and for all! In **igniting a profound inner revolution**, and having made a leap out of our painful pasts, we have opened the way for grace to thrust us further. **As mature, wiser, and spiritually centered adults we take full responsibility now, to take ownership, and to continue to evolve.**

With the following stabilizing practices you can move into God-mind, or Buddha-mind, or Mary-mind, or Tao-mind, whatever you call it, more quickly. Now you will get to give those intuitive muscles a frequent workout in the gym of your mind and heart. When you are in tune, you will hear a clear voice of guidance. Sometimes it will whisper and sometimes it will roar. Your conscious breathing will help you to get into the meditative zone quickly, no matter where you are. If you need to make a decision, the answer will come. Or the message will say, "not now," or "wait," or "pray more into this one." And *that*, my friends, is powerful living—**true, authentic, powerful living**.

This level of conscious awareness makes you feel **confident, bold, wise, and loving** at the right times. It can help you know when to keep your mouth shut and when you should speak up. It helps you to know when to listen more, work harder, mobilize, or to ask for help. It helps to remember to let go and surrender. It helps you draw those healthy boundaries with clients, friends, family, and even strangers at the right times.

Now I know that my **intuition**, my **God-self**, wants me to value my physical body, my whole being, and the whole of life. Spirit wants me to make choices that affirm my good, others' good, and to be prosperous. It wants me to speak my mind, to confront when I need to confront, and to demand justice when I need to. It helps me stop to breathe into potentially stressful situations. It helps me know that being pretty is not my function in the world as I was taught as a little girl. It helps me know I am beautiful and brilliant just as I am. It helps me stay away from many negative things and people. Mostly it helps me shift my mind into awareness, and joy, and feeling free. It helps me know I am safe, loved, and loving. It says, **"Girl, you need to dance, now!"** It says, **"You have enough, ENOUGH, E.N.O.U.G.H. Be humble. Be grateful!"**

Pause for a moment and consider what your intuition might be saying to you right now.

"Ego-identification with things creates attachment to things, obsession with things, which in turn creates our consumer society and economic structures where the only measure of progress is always more. The unchecked striving for more, for endless growth, is a dysfunction and a disease."
—*Eckhart Tolle*

When I hear others say, "Oh you are so Pollyanna," or "You are too positive," I think, "Do they really believe that?" Being positive does not mean denying anything. There is no denial going on here. **Being happy, positive, and at peace requires work.** But I embrace the work as a fun challenge, and it actually gets easier in a lot of ways; but it's not as if there is no work involved. Have you had similar experiences where people have tried to deny your positive attitude? What did it feel like? How might you respond differently to that kind of negativity now? I have even seen some people who appear to seek satisfaction in the "suffering of life." They are the ones who have said the "Pollyanna" comments to me. Yes, people suffer. We all do, but even the great Buddhas teach that **life is to find and be joy.** State aloud, **"Life is to find and be joy."** Say it again, and really own it this time.

Choosing positively and being spiritually centered is a healthy way of being in the world. In my practice I don't advocate denying the negative, dark, ugly parts of life, but I don't like seeing people stuck there. That is why I have given you tools to help you move with and through things as much as I can. Please use these tools to help others where you can. We can bless others and pray for others. We can volunteer in service. Our profession can be a type of service. We can hold immense compassion for those who seem stuck in suffering. We can offer a hand and donate and take action. We can be philanthropic. We must not let ourselves rid ourselves of happiness because others are stuck. And we must not let ourselves become condescending or rude about—or unaware of—these things. Your intuition will guide you as to the right course of action or non-action for you at any given time. Be true to what feels good to you, draw healthy boundaries as to how much and how often you say "yes" or "no" to a person or situation. And remember if anyone is being verbally aggressive, physically abusive, or hurtful to you, you can simply walk away and send prayers or silent blessings.

"It isn't the things that happen
to us in our lives that cause
us to suffer, it's how we relate
to the things that happen to
us that causes us to suffer."
—*Pema Chodron*

This process is about dealing with all of it—embracing it, loving it, and releasing it. That is what leads to your stabilized presence and stronger intuition and prosperity consciousness. You can begin to move past the hardened boulders and rough edges of life like water. Be aware. Stay alert. Stay awake. And let life flow. You have a plethora of resources you can integrate into your inner guidance system to get you out of the dark. Your new inner resources will help to limit your wandering missteps and liquefy your sense of energy.

NALU (MEDITATION) AND PULE (PRAYER)

Nalu and prayer are the two most important stabilizing practices I know of that can help to bring your life into oneness with your divinity. You have worked with this a bit already, but now you can understand these practices at deeper levels. They are integral to living a spirit filled and purposeful life. With regular practice they can help you reap more peace and have even less stress in all areas of your life. They can be performed alone or with others. They can be done at any time and location. Consider these as part of your daily spiritual commute. Your commitment to them is the hard part. Having faith in the practices to change your life and witnessing change in your life will help you keep up and keep going, and they will become ingrained in you as healthy habit. If you do not pray and meditate to deepen your spiritual practice, you suffer when you do not get what you want in the world. But as you have met the essence of spirit, it will not matter if you don't get your way. Even if people say or do things that are crazy, upsetting, and hurtful—you can smile and be peaceful anyway.

NALU

I have been asking you to notice your breathing throughout this book with intentions of inviting you to try a committed meditation practice. Meditation is a common spiritual practice across the globe and within many belief systems and religions. The aim of meditation is to help you arrive at a deeper order of reality. It can also be a complex study and a complex practice.

Simply put, meditation is a mindful practice of returning to your breath to remind you to be aware of what you are thinking so that you can let go of thinking and move into a deeper space, being at one with your defined Source. It helps you become an outside observer of your ego. It is about quieting yourself even if there is noise all around you. It is about returning to the silence and peace that is already within you. It is also a type of **self focus** that can come without much or any effort on your part. **Seemingly out of nowhere, wisdom, answers, and insights come.** Meditation can help you sit with your upset to find profound teachings and insights, or to appreciate your gifts and the gifts of life. In his book *The Energy of Prayer,* the Vietnamese Buddhist Thich Nhat Hanh tells us,

> *"Meditation is particularly able to help us with internal*
> *knots and identity complexes. These fetters keep us*
> *from being able to be in the present moment."*

Here are a few pointers for a sitting meditation practice:

1. Prepare your surroundings with a comfortable sitting area. You can use a traditional cushion or whatever feels good to you. Early morning before others are awake is a prime time to meditate. If you cannot do it in the morning, then do it before going to bed. Ideally, you could do both.

2. Ensure a quiet space without television, phones, or loud noises of any kind. Let others know they should not disturb you for at least thirty minutes. Allow someone to enter into the space only when the time is up. You could also set a low volume alarm to ensure your time frame. Certain background noises are unavoidable so ignore them.

3. You could light a candle or place a photo of something inspiring in front of you. It is okay to have nothing or a blank wall in front of you also.

4. Once you are seated, begin to gently move your shoulders up and down a few times to help you relax, and start to consciously let go of any outside stressors such as noise in the room, street noise, alarms,

loud voices, or traffic. Let go of anything else you suddenly think you should be doing or what you are going to do when you are done. Stay present and in the moment.

5.   Affirm this sacred inner time for yourself. Give silent statements of gratitude or begin by saying a prayer of gratitude aloud.

6.   Then slowly become quiet and silent.

7.   Let your eyes softly close like baby eyes falling asleep (but do not let yourself fall asleep).

8.   Breathe in through the nose and out through the mouth.

9.   Continue to let thoughts drift by in your mind's eye.

10. It is likely that your mind will wander before you really even get started. You might think of the dust bunny in the corner you noticed earlier. You might think you have no time for this "doing nothing." You might think about what you want for dinner, or tomorrow's dinner, or the dog's dinner. You might think about the indigestion you will get if you opt for greasy foods versus something more healthy—like, say, organic brown rice and broccoli but then you think that just sounds so boring. You might remember you forgot to call someone. You might consider a quadratic equation. You might find yourself on any number of topics that just keep your mind spinning. THIS IS NORMAL. Let your inner Buddha have a good giggle for a moment.

11. Just keep trying to focus on your breathing and start over. Keep returning to the breath.

12. If you wish, focus on a short mantra such as "I am an instrument of peace." Let all other thoughts go.

13. If you do not choose a mantra, that is fine.

14. Allow spirit to breathe you. Surrender to breathing.

15. Relax, let thoughts go, just breathe.

16. At some point you may feel like you are melting into oneness with spirit. Note the sensation, and don't get lost in thinking. Return to breathing. See if any answers come to you. See if spirit has any messages or inspirations for you. If so, just note them and return to breathing until your time is up.

Meditation can also help you hold **compassion,** and to understand differences. It is important not to judge yourself in meditation. In the practice, you release those thoughts, and simply breathe. It is about **going with the flow of breathing, and just being, as in existing.** Meditation is a practice that was used by Jesus and Buddha. It continues to be used by Christians, Sufis, Kabbalists, Zen and Tibetan Buddhists, Hindu Yogis, Taoists, and many more. It is a practice of returning to a **stable state,** or a state of equilibrium. The more you take the time to go into the silence, the more centered you become and therefore able to handle life's changes, and stresses, better. There is nothing magical about it, and there is no secret to it. It is about **quieting the mind**. You notice the thoughts, then let them go, and you open to answers that you are seeking.

I once heard that prayer is a method of asking God for help, and meditation is the method by which the answers come.

There are many ways to meditate and there are many articles, books, and classes one could take, and I highly encourage you to do so if it feels right to you. You do not have to go to a church or to a temple, mosque, or meditation center. You can be at home, in bed, walking, on a bus or train, at work—the location doesn't matter. I have taken a few meditation classes over the years, and I have learned to integrate the teachings of several masters. My regular practice consists of daily mindfulness in all that I do including when I wash the dishes, brush my teeth, when I'm in the shower, gardening, or folding clothes. I typically sit on my cushion or up in bed for about fifteen to thirty minutes of meditation at night, and ten to twenty minutes in the morning. I incorporate silence and verbal prayer. There are times when I do more, especially if I feel troubled over something or even when I feel an overwhelming sense of gratitude.

"Be master of mind rather than mastered by the mind."
—*Zen Proverb*

"Life is the companion of death; death is the beginning of life. Who can understand how the two are related? We arrive here from them unknown and go back to where we are from. What people love about life is its miraculous beauty; what they hate about death is the loss and decay around it. Yet losing is not losing and decay turns into beauty, as beauty turns back into decay. We are breathed in, breathed out. Therefore all you need is to understand the one breath."

—*Chuang Tzu*

I love the teachings of Thich Nhat Hanh, a Vietnamese Buddhist Monk who imparts Zen teachings with social activism. I also include Eight Point Passage Meditation from Eknath Easawaran from Southern India, with the mindfulness based stress reduction practices of Jon Kabat-Zinn, a Western medical doctor. More recently I have meditated with Adyashanti at the lovely Spirit Rock meditation center in Northern California.

When I first began to meditate, I listened to Dr. Wayne Dyer's CDs titled "Meditations for Manifesting," "Change Your Thoughts" (based on the Tao), and Dr. Deepak Chopra's CD, "The Soul of Healing Meditations." I continue to try new ways of getting into the meditative zone. I can also find myself in a meditative zone during gentle yoga, while sipping tea, during nature walks, while cooking or prepping foods, journaling, brushing my teeth, showering, bathing, and even while cleaning the house.

PULE

Pule (prayer) is the second stabilizing practice to help you **maintain your connection with your highest self**. There are two elements of effective prayer: relationship and energy. Relationship is about who you pray to with an inter-connection of communication. The energy is like an electric current—love, mindfulness, concentration, and being in the present moment can be seen as levels of energy. When your body and mind are tuned in and dwelling in this space you attain insight and wisdom.

As you can guess from earlier chapters, I am not talking about the bargaining, begging, and beseeching type of prayer to an external God such as to the white bearded man in the sky that many of us learned about from our well-intended parents and religious communities. I am talking about a positive practical spiritual prayer practice. You can use any type that feels right for you, of course. But having immersed myself in the Unity teachings, and having become a Unity Prayer Chaplain, I can tell you that this type of prayer resonates with a lot of people, including Christians, Jews, and others. The urge to pray is universal. People pray when they are happy and sad, in times of peace and in war. People pray at births and at deaths. People pray in churches, cathedrals, in times of financial strife, and when they win the lottery. Some

"Faith shows us that we are never alone. Transformation helps us to be the mystery."
—*Paulo Coelho*

cultures pray to ancestors. In the various forms of prayer, including chanting, singing psalms and hymns, meditation and mindfulness, all across the globe, people close their eyes, kneel, bow, and join hands.

The type of prayer I use is inclusive, and it is a heart-centered practice. It is a type of prayer using your highest inner powers, with spirit energy moving in, through, and *as* you, as a powerful source of good, healing, and miracles. Prayer helps you commune with the Absolute. Life affirming prayer teaches you to be grateful, to affirm the good, to forgive, to believe, to know healing potentials, and to claim right-mindedness. When you pray for others or for yourself, you lift up requests for prayer to their full healing capacity.

As a chaplain, I learned that we hold **no doubts** for one's healing potential or for any prayer. We affirm the good, even through what seems to be bad, such as a poor diagnosis or prognosis. We affirm the body, mind, and soul as having full healing power. We affirm healing even through a divorce, illness, a layoff, or a death. With positive life affirming prayer, we hold a high-energy space for God to be present—to work in and through us. We hold the same potential for others as well. By doing so, we are choosing to act and think from the space from which spirit thinks. Said another way, this is an act of oneness with divine mind and affirming the God powers within each of us. We also release the prayer and note that all answers are on God's time. We release our agenda and expectations about the outcomes, staying open to the forms they may come in. Prayer builds faith, and faith takes us more deeply into who we really are.

Below are some examples of positive life affirming prayer. Real names have been withheld to retain confidentiality.

"Mother, Father, God, Divine Presence, thank you for this new moment. Let us consciously breathe together as we honor the prayer request from Jane. We take three deep breaths as we ground into this sacred time together. Let us release any un-forgiveness we may be holding on to. We release negativity, doubts, and worries as we settle

into this prayer. Spirit, Jane has brought forth a prayer to heal the disconnection with her son, Robert. We acknowledge the hurt and pain in both of these beautiful children of God, and we pray for a healing to occur so they may reunite as mother to son and son to mother. We absolutely see and know the potential for a loving re-connection. Jane has expressed her desire to have her son home for the holidays. We pray for divine ideas and divine intervention to come, so that they can come together again, to reunite to enjoy the holiday season together. We envision them laughing and smiling with a loving hug reunion. Wherever her son is at this time, we send him immense love and we see joy on his face. We see him surrounded by the light of God, and safe. We give thanks for knowing thy will is done. We lovingly release this prayer to the universe, and know that the healing is already on its way to Jane and her Robert by whatever way Source sees fit, and on God's time line. We envision Jane being able to move through the days with God's love in her heart, and staying open to miracles. We give immense appreciation from deep within our hearts. Thank you, thank you, thank you, spirit. And so it is. Amen."

"God, thank you for this opportunity to connect in prayer. Thank you for dreaming me, sleeping, waking, praying, and breathing me. I affirm that breath is the miracle of my life. I affirm this day to be full of divine creative ideas, and I have the talent, skills, energy, and focus to carry them through. I affirm the good in myself and in all people. I am inspired by life. I consciously step into this day aligned with one Divine Mind—in, through, and as me. And so it is. Amen."

"Divine Presence, thank you for my beautiful body. I see and know that my cells are active, alive, and thriving. My body is a sacred temple, and I feed my body the most alive and healthy foods to sustain my right thinking and my high energy. I am grateful for my job, family,

and friends. I appreciate having the ability to move my limbs, and to walk gracefully into this day prepared to work and serve others with my unique talents and skills. What a gift it is to feel my body and to use it for health and healing on the planet. Thank you, spirit. And so it is. Amen."

"Holy Spirit, I come to thee for prayer for a dear friend, Kelly. I affirm that beautiful healing white light surrounds her and holds her peacefully as she mourns the loss of her beloved husband, George. I affirm that this light of peace is moving in and around her even though she may not sense it at this time. She is held in the love of God. She is surrounded by loving souls to hold and nurture her. And as surely as each day breaks, she is moving through her pain and suffering, and her grief and loss. She is in a divine process of healing, and it is right and perfect. I release this prayer to the divine. Thank you, thank you, thank you. And so it is. Amen."

"Spirit, I come to thee in time of need. I have tried many ways and I feel lost. I have not been living from my highest self. I need to get back on course. So now, I consciously return home to my good, to peace, to right mind. I affirm my oneness with thee. I affirm forgiveness and step into my fullness. I breathe in and out, slowly, as I plug back into my Source. I surrender to the divine order. I absolutely know that the answers that I seek are on their way to me. I am bathed in love and I am kissed on the forehead by wise saints and sages. I stay open to miracle moments and am blissfully aware of nature all around me. I am being re-birthed as I imagine a new flower budding. I am a child of the divine, and I step out of the dark and into the light. Releasing this prayer to Source, I say thank you. And so it is. Amen."

"Beloved, I know angels are watching over my mother. She is held in a glowing, loving embrace of divine energy. She is at peace as she sleeps, as she wakes, and as she moves through her days. She is safe, calm, and smiling. I affirm her pure love and sweetness. I see and know that my mother's life is full of abundance. She is abundant with energy, with life, with love, with kindness, with joy, and with money. She is wealthy beyond measure. My mother is loved and adored. Thank you, thank you, thank you. And so it is. Amen."

"Spirit, please be with my dear aunt. She is need of support and peace. As I bring her face into my mind's eye, I note her strength and her character. I peer deeply into her eyes with a sense of peace and serenity. I affirm healing in her heart, and in her whole being. I affirm that she is comforted. I hold her in the highest regard, and I know the hospice workers are indeed comforting her and keeping her pain free. Thank you for the hospice workers. We know their hearts and that every action they take is full of love. Thank you for all of the memories. I affirm that her love lasts forever. I release this prayer to God. And so it is. Amen."

"Vast and mysterious Source, thank you for the rains that are pouring down drenching the earth today. I love to note the nourishment, the cleansing, and the filling up. Thank you for the gorgeous pine trees, and the oak trees, and the farms, and the gardens. Thank you so much for the singing birds and the rainbows. Thank you for the return of the sunshine. I am grateful and so full, also cleansed, by the fresh air and the coolness. I bless this earth, my home. Thank you for this amazing planet, and beyond. And so it is. Amen."

For four years, I led the annual New Year's Eve Day World Healing Meditation event at Unity of Berkeley. The event started in 1986 and is connected to a worldwide mind link. Millions of people join in at noon Greenwich time in the early morning hours of New Years Eve Day to participate. In Berkeley, California, this meant I had to wake up at 3 A.M. to be there at 4 A.M. to lead the event. It was very rewarding to participate with such a huge group of global citizens, consciously connecting, to help heal the planet. This was more rewarding than any New Years Eve Party I ever attended. Below is part of the shared prayer reading:

> *"The one Light of Love, Peace, and Understanding is moving. It flows across the face of the earth. Touching and illuminating every soul in the shadow of the illusion. And where there was darkness, there is now the Light of Reality.*
>
> *I am seeing the salvation of the planet before my very eyes, as all false beliefs and error patterns are dissolved. The sense of separation is no more; the healing has taken place, and the world is restored to sanity.*
>
> *This is the beginning of Peace on Earth and Good Will toward all, as Love flows forth from every heart, forgiveness reigns in every soul, and all hearts and minds are in perfect understanding. It is done. And it is so."*

EXERCISE

Create your own positive prayer for something you need in your life right now. Either journal it or say it out loud.

EXERCISE

Create an altar in your home. This can be on one single shelf, or a mantle, or the corner of a desk. Decorate with objects that feel sacred to you such photos or statues. You may want to add a candle or a flower. You could also place a few of your favorite affirmations there—a prayer, a poem, a photo of your guru, or mentor, or a piece of art.

You don't have to wait for an annual event to begin your stabilizing practices. Prayer and meditation allow you to relax into sensations of your body and to surrender to the consciousness of eternal present moments no matter where you are. Yoga also incorporates prayer in a number of ways.

If we choose not to pray and deny the opportunity to deepen our spiritual practices, we end up suffering when things don't go our way. But if we stay in these practices, then when things go wrong we don't care if we get our way or not. It just doesn't matter because we can tap back into the peace, the comfort, and joy that is always available. The lesson is pretty clear here—stay prayed up.

Near your altar, create a place where you can sit to pray or meditate regularly. As you engage with the above practice, sit in a comfortable position, with your palms facing up. Close your eyes, and begin to notice your breath. Just breathe naturally. Then focus on breathing in through your nose and out through your mouth. Let those thoughts go.

Just breathe. If you experience any physical pain, notice it, send a conscious breath to that spot, then let it go. Keep returning to breathing. Try not to over-think this practice. Just try it. Be kind to yourself.

You do not need to be a monk and go sit in a cave to meditate or pray. You do not need to shave your head or sell all of your possessions, or start to wear different clothes. Put your energy into sitting quietly and focus on your breathing. Let the state of continual presence become your normal every day state of being. **Let love find a home in your being, and let yourself open to divine awareness.**

For the above practice, use any method that is comfortable to you. If you cannot commit to the practice at this time, then a simple gratitude prayer at the beginning and end of your day might feel like enough. Just listen to that **one true inner voice** and you will know what to pray about and for how long to meditate.

EXERCISE

I call this "The Sitting Challenge." For thirty days, commit to a regular sitting meditation or prayer practice, or both, at least one hour per day—you can break it up into thirty minutes in the morning, and thirty minutes in the evening. The goal is to experiment and eventually commit to a regular practice as often as you can. You may want to start each session with a spoken prayer, then move into silence with meditation.

EXERCISE

If you need to, this is a good time to go back to chapter 11 and re-evaluate where you are on your spiritual path. The questions in that chapter will help you see how far you've come, and where you might still want to go.

CHAPTER 23: ESSENTIAL QUESTIONS

As the master of your life—you are your own CLO (Chief Life Officer), co-creating with the divine—you can reap significant rewards. In this chapter you are asked to familiarize yourself with a list of essential questions you can practice asking every day until they become ingrained in your thinking and applied when making any kind of choice. You can use your prayer to ask your Source for the answers; then, when you are silent with meditation, you might receive answers. Of course the answers may come at any time. Stay tuned in. The questions will help guide you to a place where you live mostly from a balanced state, with more freedom to be who you are. Notice what your ego might say versus what your soul says as you ask the questions. Use these questions to give yourself even more personal power and meaning in your life. I learned some of these from the Undisputed Life-Coaching Master, Tony Robbins.

Ask these questions earnestly for at least one day. And notice how you will likely make different choices. If it feels right, keep them so they become automatic questions for daily living. Allow your intuitive response to take precedence over any other option that might surface in your mind.

EXERCISE

Think of a choice you need to make and ask yourself the following questions.

1. Is this choice going to advance me toward living the life I dream of, or will it keep me stuck in the past?

2. With this choice, am I standing in my power or just trying to please someone else?

3. Will this choice add to my life force, or will it rob me of my sacred energy?

4. Will I use this choice, or situation, as a catalyst to grow and evolve, or will I use it to undermine myself?

5. Does this choice empower me, or does it rob me of my authentic power?

6. With this choice, am I acting from self-love (in the best sense of this term), or am I sabotaging myself?

7. Am I choosing from love, or fear?

8. Am I choosing from my divinity, or from my lower self?

"The only valuable
thing is intuition."
—*Albert Einstein*

As you build your intuition, you will live more from your truth. **Stay loyal to yourself** and do not emulate others. Stay in the powerful zone of being your true self. You cannot control others, but you can control yourself and your mind. You can control your choices and your behaviors. Stay in your authentically powerful zone. **You are the master of your own fate, the captain of your soul, of the ship of you.** Be the excellence you know you are capable of. Practice everywhere you go. You can practice being able to perform at higher levels of energy for longer periods of time. Remember, if you make a mistake, acknowledge it, then let it go. Just keep trying, learning, growing, and having fun.

This love that shines, this love that you are, this is the deepest part of you. You are radiating and you are liberating!

"Dying is no big deal.
Living is the trick."
—*Red Smith*

CHAPTER 24: HONORING YOURSELF

Congratulations on working through this book and developing a new relationship with your life! You have been consciously opening the doorway to living from a higher place within and allowing grace to flow in, through, and as you. You have the tools to create a conscious relationship with the deeper order of reality and to open up to more divine creativity. Not many people get around to even thinking about their life purpose much less to consciously creating it. The world needs more people like you.

It is important to **celebrate yourself and your life on a regular basis.** I encourage you to find reasons to celebrate even the smallest success that you achieve, and to acknowledge this in others as well.

Try this visualization: Close your eyes and really feel into this. Breathe. Notice nature all around you, and feel with all your senses. **Relax into the oneness** of life. Feel the cells in your body becoming more engaged and turned on with the energy of life all around you. As you feel the energy, surrender to the vibrations and the interconnection of things. Feel your heart beating from the center of your being. Notice concentric circles of energy emanating out from your heart center. Affirm the talent, the **brilliance**, the **inventiveness**, and the **brightness** of your being. **Breathe** into the knowing that **all is well.**

Affirm your legacy. Affirm your life purpose. Breathe. Sink further into your essence. Be here now. Breathe into the silence for about ten minutes. Then turn your attention to the poem on page 274. Read each line slowly and contemplatively.

EXERCISE

Designate some special time to reassert your identity and appreciate yourself in the form of a ritual or ceremony. This can be very simple, yet meaningful. See below for ideas and further instructions.

"We are all Bodhisattvas.
There is nothing to do.
You are already there.
You are beauty.
The truth is non-duality.
There is neither 2 nor 1.
You are already totally
complete, full and rich.

It is done.
And simultaneously this apparent spirit and human journey will unfold this. The journey is the only way to manifest. There is goodness all the way through!"
—*Adyashanti*

Ho'olaile'a (celebrating) your evolvement is important, and I encourage you to hold a type of celebration for yourself. This can include a small intimate gathering or a larger party but it does not have to be elaborate. Celebrations and rituals can be simple. A celebration marks an event and honors it with your attention. A celebration ritual can be as simple as lighting a candle and making a statement of intention, saying an affirmation, a prayer, or a gratitude blessing. You could make a cup of tea and listen to inspiring music. You can enjoy celebrating alone or with friends.

Find a creative way to incorporate your framed life purpose and passion statement you made in Chapter 19. For example, read it out loud and pass it around to those you may have invited to your celebration. Even if the celebration is for yourself only, read it to yourself. Honor it. Honor yourself and the meaning and commitment you have made.

Here are some more examples:

- Plant a tree in your honor. There is a wonderful organization in Hawaii where you can help reforest Hawaii by donating a tree in someone's name. Check out http://www.legacytrees.org. For those not in Hawaii here is another good resource: http://www.arborday.org/programs/trees4america.cfm

- Plant a flower in your honor.

- Host a small brunch or dinner.

- Buy a nice candle in your honor and light it.

- Make a visit to a special place in nature, in your honor.

- Hike a mountain, in your honor.

- Buy a new journal, in your honor.

- Give a gift to a noble cause, in your name.

- Enjoy a celebration picnic with a few friends.

- Ask a few close trusted friends (who you know will support you on your journey) to join you for a "stepping into my light" party. Use your imagination. Make it up! Use art, poetry, music, candles, dance... whatever resonates with you.

- I cannot go without suggesting a Hawaiian luau theme! Improvise this in any way.

- Incorporate the following Hawaiian chants into an honoring ritual. Don't worry about pronunciation, but research it if you wish, or use the English version I have provided below.

   "Owau no ka 'Ho,' a meka 'ha.'"

   Translation: "I am the incoming and the outgoing of breath."

   "Puamaianmaikapoiloko o kamalalalama,"

   Translation: "I come forth from the void into the light."

"Grace comes into the soul, as the morning sun into the world: first a dawning, then a light, and at last the sun in his full and excellent brightness."
—*Thomas Adams*

CHAPTER 25: THANK YOU

Mahalo nui loa (thank you very much) for your energy and your light. I acknowledge your choice to pick up this book. **I celebrate you and I appreciate you.** I also remind you, gently, to **always remain grateful for life—appreciate all of it**. Love your legacy. Live your legacy. Leave your legacy. It takes guts, grit, and grace to follow your heart and to create the life you dream of living. Have fun. It's okay to become a workafrolic to make your dreams come true! Don't lose faith and don't settle. Reinvent as many times as you need to. Stay focused, practice, and persist. Tame your ego. You are here to manifest your greatness!

Enjoy the following poem and prayer, with aloha. You may wish to use these in your celebration.

The Sea

"I need the sea because it teaches me.
I don't know if I learn music or awareness, if it's a single wave or its vast
existence, or only its harsh voice or its shining suggestion of fishes and ships.
The fact is that until I fall asleep, in some magnetic way
I move in the university of the waves.
It's not simply the shells crunched as if some shivering planet were giving signs
of its gradual death;
No, I reconstruct the day out of a fragment, the stalactite from a sliver of salt,
and the great god out of a spoonful.
What it taught me before, I keep.
It's air, ceaseless wind, water and sand.
It seems a small thing for a young man, to have come here to live with his own
fire; nevertheless,
the pulse that rose and fell in its abyss,
the crackling of the blue cold, the gradual wearing of the star, the soft unfolding
of the wave squandering snow with its foam, the quiet power out there, sure as a
stone shrine in the depths, replaced my world in which were growing stubborn
sorrow, gathering oblivion, and my life changed suddenly:
as I became part of its pure movement."

—Pablo Neruda

EXERCISE

Affirm the following

A Prayer for All

"Dear Source, thank you for life, love, and legacy. Thank you for the ability to share and inspire one another through our creativity energy, our collective soul consciousness. Let us affirm that we all know, without any doubts, our own deep, blue heavenly seas—the truth and purpose of our being. We claim it and name it in our own words, rowing our own boat, on our own course, for the greater good of all. We say "Mahalo" often. We feel Pele burning in our belly, and in the belly of all of life. We now live our ho'oilina (legacy) and practice our kuleana (sacred responsibility) as heirs and heiresses of the divine. We know when to take our soul on retreat so we will continue to stay programmed into spirit. We are forever connected to all in a sea of love. We continue to dive in deep and ride those waves of life all the way to the shore and back again, and again. In our miracle moments, miracle movement, and miracle mindfulness we live life as a prayer, already answered. With overflowing hearts, thank you, thank you, thank you for all that is." —**And so it is. Amen.**

SUGGESTED READING

Ano Ano: The Seed, Kristen Zambucka

Awakening Joy: 10 Steps to Happiness, James Baraz and Shoshana Alexander

The Biology of Belief: Unleashing the Power of Consciousness, Matter & Miracles, Bruce H. Lipton, Ph.D.

Change Your Thoughts, Change Your Life: Living the Wisdom of the Tao, Dr. Wayne W. Dyer

Discover the Power Within You: A Guide to the Unexplained Depths Within, Eric Butterworth

Faith: Trusting Your Own Deepest Experience, Sharon Salzberg

Feel the Fear and Do It Anyway: Dynamic Techniques for Turning Fear, Indecision, and Anger into Power, Action, and Love, Susan Jeffers, Ph.D.

Forgiveness: The Greatest Healer of All, Gerald G. Jampolsky, M.D.

The Gift of Change: Spiritual Guidance for Living Your Best Life, Marianne Williamson

How Do I Live When I Know I Am Going to Die? Thoughts and Insights about Life's Most Challenging Passage and America's Last Taboo, Rev. Anton Crosz, Ph.D.

Inspiration: Your Ultimate Calling, Wayne W. Dyer

Life Lessons: Two Experts on Death and Dying Teach Us about the Mysteries of Life and Living, Elisabeth Kubler-Ross and David Kessler

A Little Book of Aloha: Spirit of Healing, Renata Provenzano

Love Is Letting Go of Fear, Gerald G. Jampolsky, M.D.

Man's Search for Meaning, Victor E. Frankl, M.D.

The Mind's Own Physician: A Scientific Dialogue with the Dalai Lama on the Healing Power of Meditation, Edited by Jon Kabat-Zinn, Ph.D. and Richard J. Davidson, Ph.D. with Zara Houshmand

A New Earth: Awakening to Your Life's Purpose, Eckhart Tolle

New Hawaiian Pocket Dictionary, Mary Kawena Pukui and Samuel H. Elbert

Pele: The Fire Goddess, Bishop Museum Press

Pele's Wish: Secrets of the Hawaiian Masters and External Life, Sondra Ray

A Return to Love: Reflections on the Principles of *A Course in Miracles*, Marianne Williamson

Spiritual Economics: The Principles and Process of True Prosperity, Eric Butterworth

There Is a Spiritual Solution to Every Problem, Wayne W. Dyer

Touching the Earth: Intimate Conversations with the Buddha, Thich Nhat Hanh

CPSIA information can be obtained
at www.ICGtesting.com
Printed in the USA
FSOW03n0732270415
6736FS

9 780986 381638